Routledge Revivals

Long Term Results of Infant School Methods

rst published in 1950, *Long Term Results of Infant School Methods* was written explain and summarise the results of Gardner's experiment to test the tent to which the effect of different styles of Infant school education, xperimental" or "control", would also be apparent at a later stage.

The book details how the tests and the schools involved were chosen; the fferent types of tests conducted and their respective aims; and a summary of ardner's conclusions. It will appeal to those with an interest in the history d theory of education.

Long Term Results of Infant School Methods

By D. E. M. Gardner

First published in 1950
by Methuen & Co. Ltd

This edition first published in 2021 by Routledge
2 Park Square, Milton Park, Abingdon, Oxon, OX14 4RN
and by Routledge
605 Third Avenue, New York, NY 10017

Routledge is an imprint of the Taylor & Francis Group, an informa business

© 1950 D. E. M. Gardner

All rights reserved. No part of this book may be reprinted or reproduced or utilised in any form or by any electronic, mechanical, or other means, now known or hereafter invented, including photocopying and recording, or in any information storage or retrieval system, without permission in writing from the publishers.

Publisher's Note
The publisher has gone to great lengths to ensure the quality of this reprint but points out that some imperfections in the original copies may be apparent.

Disclaimer
The publisher has made every effort to trace copyright holders and welcomes correspondence from those they have been unable to contact.

ISBN 13: 978-1-032-00174-6 (hbk)
ISBN 13: 978-1-003-17306-9 (ebk)

Book DOI: 10.4324/9781003173069

LONG TERM RESULTS OF INFANT SCHOOL METHODS

by

D. E. M. GARDNER
M.A.
HEAD OF THE DEPARTMENT OF CHILD DEVELOPMENT,
UNIVERSITY OF LONDON INSTITUTE OF EDUCATION

WITH 16 ILLUSTRATIONS

METHUEN & CO. LTD. LONDON
36 Essex Street, Strand, W.C.2

First published in 1950

CATALOGUE NO. 5332/U

PRINTED IN GREAT BRITAIN

PREFACE

IN MY former book, "Testing Results in the Infant School," I attempted to evaluate the achievements of children in Infant schools - where, to quote Susan Isaacs, "the children were allowed to move and talk and play" as compared with those of children educated in a more formal and traditional way. I called the former type of school "experimental" and the latter, "control," since my purpose was to measure the effects upon the children in the more modern type of Infant School by the yardstick of what was commonly achieved in the more conventional type of school.

I tested the children towards the end of their Infant school period, both for their attitudes to school life and work and for their attainments in "subjects" of the Infant school curriculum. I intended to carry on the study to include eight-year-old children during their first year in the Junior school, but owing to the outbreak of war and the consequent scattering of the children, I was able to test the children aged eight in only one pair of schools.

The differences between the performance of children aged seven in Infant schools where education was based on their spontaneous interests as compared with that of children in more formal Infant schools were so marked, in certain respects, that I became very interested in the problem of how far such differences would be apparent at a later stage.

In 1944, when I came to London, it seemed possible to begin again, using fresh schools, including some in the north of England where methods had changed and which, therefore, gave me the opportunity of testing in the same schools nine-year-old children who had come from formal Infant schools before the change was made and repeating the tests when these children were replaced by nine-year-olds who had received a more informal Infant school education.

vi LONG TERM TESTING IN INFANT SCHOOL

This plan had the advantage that the children would probably have had the same teachers for both methods, but the disadvantage that the lapse of several years would possibly present other inequalities, especially if the standard of feeding and general conditions of living had improved or deteriorated.

In fact another difficulty arose in that so many changes of staff took place in the interval between the administration of tests to the control groups and to the experimental, that the anticipated advantage was largely lost. Moreover, I found that as a result of experience it became evident that the method of administering the tests and the actual content of certain tests needed more modification than I had allowed for, to make them fully satisfactory for older children, so that the value of the work carried out between January 1944 and July 1946 was largely that of a pilot study, and little value could be ascribed to the actual results. Some tests were found to have been too easy and others too difficult, with the result that in many cases equality of result was inevitable. Moreover, owing to the increase in my commitments in London, I was unable in 1946 to administer the tests myself to the experimental groups in the North of England and had to delegate this work to another tester, which is never wholly satisfactory in a comparative study, however closely one attempts to standardise procedure. The personality of the tester is liable to affect certain results.

I decided, therefore, to begin the work again in 1947, using the same testers for each pair of schools, modifying tests where experience proved it desirable, and attempting to find schools where staffing changes had been less frequent although so universal has been the problem of the shifting of staffs that it was not possible to secure anything like entire stability in the type of Infant and Junior School education which the children had received, and in this respect the first set of results described in this volume (i.e. those of the nine-year-old children) is less satisfactory than that of my former investigation. In one case it was

PREFACE   vii

possible to find the experimental and control groups in the
same Junior School, but in most cases the children from
the experimental and control Infant Schools entered different Junior Schools, so it was impossible to eliminate
the possibility that some differences might have been due
to the Junior School influence rather than the long-distance
effect of the Infant School.   Care was, however, taken to
select efficient Junior Schools which did not differ very
widely from each other in educational procedure and where
the teachers were not too varied in ability.   On the whole
they were good schools of a traditional type.

The words " experimental " and " control " as applied to
Junior Schools in this book do not, therefore, denote difference of method in the Junior Schools themselves, but
refer to the fact that the schools had received children from
Infant schools of the " experimental " or " control " type.

Because the problem of making sure that one set of
teachers was not more able than the other was so important,
it was a great disappointment that my wish to test children
taught by the same teachers using the two different methods
had to be abandoned.

It is very unlikely however, that the quality of the teachers
could have been very different; the Infant Schools concerned
were all considered " good " schools by their authorities, and
the teachers were not specially selected, nor had they, on
the whole, chosen to work in the school concerned because
of the methods carried out.*   In many cases the changes in
curriculum had come about after their appointment.   Two
of the control schools of my first research subsequently

*Critics of my former book have sometimes suggested that
the home background of children whose parents chose to
send them to an " Experimental " school was likely to be
different from those who chose a " Control " school.   In fact,
however, very few parents selected the schools for reasons of
the methods used.   Proximity of the school to the home was
the main factor which affected attendance and the children
may fairly be described as a random sample of those who
lived in a certain neighbourhood.

viii LONG TERM TESTING IN INFANT SCHOOL

changed their methods and the same teachers proved their ability to do good work on the " Experimental " lines.

During 1947-48, while the work with nine-year-olds was being carried out, a pilot study was made with ten-year-old children, and in 1948-49 tests were administered to ten-year-old children. It was also possible in that year to use some schools where staffing changes had been less frequent.

The account which follows is of the work of these two years. The first two years' pilot study showed superiority of the experimental schools in the tests for ingenuity and for concentration on a task of the children's own choice, and a less marked superiority of the control schools in some of the tests in written English. Otherwise the actual results were inconclusive; but when full enquiries were made it was found that staff changes at the Infant school stage had in many cases made it doubtful whether all the experimental Infant Schools had in fact carried out a characteristic and stable programme during the whole period of the children's attendance.

D.E.M.G.

ACKNOWLEDGMENTS

I WISH to acknowledge gratefully much generous help from many experienced teachers who assisted me with this work while taking an advanced course of study in the Department of Child Development. Without their help I could not have completed this investigation.

Particular thanks are due to Miss Joyce Haworth, Miss Elizabeth Bradburn, Miss Ivy Davis, Miss Ruth Bakewell, Miss Barbara Smith and Miss Elese Murray, who administered tests and recorded the children's responses.

Many other colleagues and members of the Department gave most valuable help by assessing, analysing and scoring various tests. I am also most grateful to my colleague, Professor P. E. Vernon for advice on the statistical methods and Miss Doris M. Lee who most generously directed the mathematical calculations and my warm thanks are also due to the staff of the many schools used in this research for their unfailing and patient co-operation and to their Education Authorities for permission to use the schools.

Others who have helped me personally or through their published work in my earlier study, of which this is the continuation, are acknowledged in my former book *Testing Results in the Infant School.*

D.E.M.G.

CONTENTS

CHAPTER		PAGE
I.	THE CHOICE OF TESTS AND SCHOOLS	1
	Reasons determining the choice of tests	1
	Selection of schools and children	4
	Notes on the schools	7
	Pilot study with ten-year-old children	11
	General comments made by examiners	13
II.	THE TESTS (GROUP A) AIMING AT ASSESSMENT OF ATTITUDES TO SCHOOL LIFE AND WORK	19
	Test I Concentration	19
	Test II Listening and Remembering	29
	Test III Ingenuity	33
	Test IV Sociability	40
	Test V Interests	44
III.	THE TESTS (GROUP B) OF CERTAIN SUBJECTS IN THE JUNIOR SCHOOL CURRICULUM	71
	Test VI Arithmetic	71
	Test VII Reading—Silent	81
	Test VIII English Composition	82
	Test IX Handwriting	95
	Test X Free Drawing	96
IV.	SUMMARY OF CONCLUSIONS	101

PLATES

The sixteen illustrations will be found together between pages 36 and 37.

CHAPTER I

THE CHOICE OF TESTS AND SCHOOLS

REASONS DETERMINING THE CHOICE OF TESTS

IN MY first investigation in which I compared the achievements of children aged $6\frac{1}{2}$-$7\frac{1}{2}$ in good Infant Schools, where the curriculum was largely based on the spontaneous interests of the children, with those in good Infant Schools of a more traditional type, I found the results which I summarised as follows :—

(a) Tests in which the experimental school children were distinctly superior.

1. Assembling material ingeniously to make interesting pictures.

2. Free drawing and painting and expressing imaginative ideas through drawing.

3. Answering specific questions asked, making good sentences, and expressing themselves spontaneously in words.

4. Showing a friendly and responsive attitude to a strange adult.

5. Good social behaviour towards other children.

6. Writing quickly and neatly at seven and eight* years old.

7. Concentration on a task of their own choice.

(b) Tests in which the experimental school children tended to be superior.

8. Concentration on a task which they are asked to do, but which is not immediately interesting.

9. Listening to and illustrating a passage read to them.

10. Writing compositions at eight* years old.
*Given in one pair of schools only.

I

2 LONG TERM TESTING IN INFANT SCHOOL

(c) Those in which there was no significant difference between the two groups.

1. Answering questions on a story read to them.
2. Defining words, naming pictured objects.
3. Working the answers to simple sums in arithmetic. (Both at seven and eight* years old.)
4. Reading (at seven and eight* years old.)

*Given in one pair of schools only.

I was anxious to investigate the question as to how far the superiority of results in the tests which had proved favourable for the informal methods would be maintained after two years in the Junior School, or whether this would be lost or the more formal methods lead to greater success in the more formal work of the large majority of Junior Schools.

I was also anxious to see whether the tests which had shown no significant difference when the children were seven would show a difference if given in a more advanced form at a later stage.

Tests were selected either because they tested qualities or attitudes towards school life and work, or because they investigated achievements in the normal curriculum of the Junior School. Some tests which I should like to have given were not feasible, because of the necessity of using schools at a long distance from the London area. London schools were evacuated during the war on so large a scale that the after effects took longer to overcome than in many other areas and changes among the staffs of London schools were therefore particularly frequent. The necessity for using distant schools eliminated the possibility of using tests for which the only satisfactory method of assessment would have been the time-sampling of individual children's behaviour.

CHOICE OF TESTS AND SCHOOLS

The tests selected were as follows :—

Group A

Tests in which the aim was assessment of attitudes towards school life and work.

I.   Concentration—three tests :—

(a)   Concentration on a task chosen by the child from among his ordinary school occupations.

(b)   Concentration on a task which was not immediately interesting to the child, but which he was asked to do in order to help the tester.

(c)   Further concentration on a set task (arithmetic) on which the child had already worked for half an hour.

II.   Listening carefully and remembering what had been read.

III.   Inventiveness or ingenuity in performing an unfamiliar task.

IV.   Sociability towards other children (given in the second year only.)

V.   Interests expressed by children in answer to the following questions :—

(a)   Things you would like to learn more about in school.

(b)   New things you would like to learn.

(c)   Things you would like to stop learning.

(d)   Ways in which you would choose to spend a gift of £1.

(e)   Ways in which you would like to spend a day in your holidays.

(f)   Places you would like to go to, and things you would like to see.

Group B

Subjects of the Junior School curriculum.

VI.   Arithmetic.

(a)   Straightforward " sums " in the four rules.

(b)   Problems.

4   LONG TERM TESTING IN INFANT SCHOOL

VII.   Reading.
  (a)   Oral (given in the first year only).
  (b)   Silent.
VIII.   Written English.
  (a)   Explaining meaning of words.
  (b)   Giving directions for reaching a landmark near the school.
  (c)   Description of the home town as for a visitor.
  (d)   Sentence building.
  (e)   Giving good descriptive words.
  (f)   Original story.
  (g)   (Optional) Original verse.
IX.   Handwriting (2nd year only)
X.   Free drawing.

SELECTION OF SCHOOLS

The schools were chosen from many parts of the country, the principles of choice being :—

(1)   That Junior Schools selected must be those which receive children from Infant Schools which are suitable as fulfilling the conditions laid down in my former book as " Experimental " and " Control " Schools.   These may be briefly summarised as follows :—

An " Experimental " School for the purpose of this research is one in which creative activity is the keynote and learning through play characteristic; where the children have not less than one hour daily of activities of their own choice; where children aged five to six study reading, writing and number only if they wish to do so; and where the rest of the curriculum is influenced by the child's spontaneous interests.

A "Control" School is one in which there is little play for children after the age of five, but systematic instruction in reading, writing and number is given from the age of five; where the children throughout the school have a well thought out and balanced curriculum planned by the teachers,

CHOICE OF TESTS AND SCHOOLS 5

but which takes less account of the spontaneous interests of the children.

Both types of school are " good " of their kind, staffed by able teachers, and where the children are happy.

2. Each experimental school was paired with one in a similiar social district and if possible in the same district; but in any case in the same town.

3. Schools were selected where the Head Teachers and staffs were generously willing to co-operate by placing the children's time at the disposal of the testers and undertaking the inconvenience of adjusting time-tables and supplying a good deal of necessary information.

4. Schools were chosen partly for their accessibility to the testers.

SELECTION OF CHILDREN

The children selected had had not less than four years of uninterrupted education, two years of which must have been in the experimental or control Infant School. Children selected were those who paired with their controls in respect of age, intelligence, sex and social background.

INTELLIGENCE TESTS AND EQUALISING OF CONDITIONS

For children who could read easily the Schonell Essential Intelligence Test was used, while for those who had difficulty in reading a non-verbal test was given. During the pilot study with nine-year-old non-readers it was found that the Pintner Cunningham Test allowed plenty of scope. The testers in the final year's work with nine-year-old children were unable to stay long enough in the areas where the schools were situated to give a non-verbal test to the children who could not read. So few nine-year-olds who were unable to read had been found in the pilot study that it did not at the time appear very serious to omit such children from the final tests, but the fact that the two schools found to contain the greatest number of non-readers were both control schools (I B and III B) may possibly have

6　LONG TERM TESTING IN INFANT SCHOOL

meant that the level of reading had been affected by over early teaching in the Infant Schools. If this was the case, it would follow that two experimental schools have been penalised by pairing for intelligence on a test involving reading. It was noticed that most of the children in Schools I A and III A who scored most highly on the Schonell Intelligence Test were not able to be paired with controls and all the work done by these children was, therefore, omitted. The difficulty was not reported to me until too late to test all the children with non-verbal tests.

The point was, however, borne in mind for the work with ten-year-old children the following year. It so happened that the two pairs of schools concerned (I A and B and III A and B) were also ones in which education in the experimental Infant Schools had been interrupted by several changes of staff. It seemed advisable therefore to omit the detailed results from these two schools for the nine-year-old year. They did not actually show very much difference between the two groups, and were very similar to those of the pilot study where staff changes had also been frequent. The results from Schools II A and B and IV A and B were much more reliable and have therefore been reported.

The comments on the children's reactions to the tests have been given in all cases, because of the light they sometimes throw on the schools concerned, which were the same schools as were used for the ten-year-olds. At the ten-year-old level five pairs of schools were able to be used.

For the ten-year-olds the Cattell non-verbal test, Scale 1, was used for children who could not read. In one pair of schools this test was used throughout, because the Schonell Test was temporarily unobtainable. Later the two tests were given to the same group of children and a fairly good correlation was found. The range of results was wide, as was to be expected, because the groups of children tested were very varied in ability. In the larger schools, the children were deliberately selected from A, B, C, and D

CHOICE OF TESTS AND SCHOOLS 7

" streams ", so that the results should be as representative as possible.

The children were paired for their scores on the test and also for age, sex and type of social background. The tests were administered in exactly the same manner in all schools and as far as possible by the same tester for each pair of schools, and at the same time of day—though some very minor variation in these matters was occasionally inevitable. Such variations were, however, very slight. The testers watched each other at work and standardised all details of procedure very carefully, so that if for reasons of expediency it was impossible for one tester to visit a school on a particular day and one or two tests had to be given by the second tester to children whose controls she had not tested, no detail of procedure would be altered. In the ten-year-old year it was found possible to use the same tester every time without a single exception.

COMMENTS MADE BY THE TESTERS WHICH MIGHT PROVE RELEVANT TO THE RESULT

" A " denotes a Junior School in which the children tested came from an Infant School using informal methods based on the children's interests. " B " denotes a Junior School in which the children came from a more formal Infant School and " A " and " B " together denote a Junior School which received children from both types of Infant School.

The numbers (i) and (ii) indicate that the school was used for the first or second year only.

School I A. A good modern building on the same site as the Infant School. One class taken by an enthusiastic but newly (" emergency ") trained man teacher. The Head Teacher expressed the view that he did not believe in cramming the children for the scholarship examination, but one class teacher expressed great enthusiasm for winning scholarships, and there was no continuity of method with the Infant School on the same site.

8   LONG TERM TESTING IN INFANT SCHOOL

I B. The school was rather overcrowded and some classes occupied temporary huts. Infant and Junior Schools were both under the same Head Teacher. In the first year one class teacher was a man awaiting training. Conditions in this school were probably not as good that year as in the Experimental school except for the possible advantages of greater continuity in the children's school life.

The school was in the same well-developed new housing estate as School I A. Both schools drew children from varied home conditions but all homes were of a good artisan type. Both schools used A, B and C categories which were all represented in the groups tested.

In both Schools I A and I B the Headmasters were friendly and co-operative with the testers, but not in sympathy with "activity methods". Both schools were overcrowded and much preparation for the scholarship examination went on.

II A. This school was in two Departments—Boys' and Girls'—and both Departments received children from both types of infant school. One Head Teacher was not in favour of the experimental methods, but said that the children from the experimental school were good at written English.

The parents were in mixed occupations, some clerks, others skilled or unskilled labourers, and a few were tradesmen.

The children mostly lived in small but well-kept houses.

III A. A very happy atmosphere. The curriculum was separated into "subjects". The children had considerable freedom and were eager to work.

Staff relationships were particularly happy.

Good work was done in Art and Craft. The building was modern, of the verandah type.

The parents were mostly in business, some were professional and a minority were small tradespeople and technicians. Many of them lived in a new housing estate and many owned or were buying their own houses. About 500

CHOICE OF TESTS AND SCHOOLS

children were on the roll of the school and there were three " streams ".

III B. (i) Staff less united. A larger school than III A and the building was not so good.

For these reasons it was decided to use another control school in the second year in which conditions would be more comparable to School III A. The parents' social background was similar to School III A.

III B. (ii) The Infant and Junior Departments were housed in the same building, but on different floors. Classrooms were light and airy with adequate space. Parents were in professions, business, clerical occupations, and a few were labourers, but the majority were technically skilled.

The school had a good atmosphere and the teaching was thorough, though with a rigid time-table and adherence to " subjects ".

IV A. Was a very good building of the verandah type, but staffing was not as good as School IV B. Methods also were more formal than in School IVB. The class tested was in the charge of a capable teacher. The curriculum was well-balanced but formal. It was on the same site as the Infant school, but conducted quite separately and without continuity in method.

The occupations of the parents varied. Some were teachers, others in business or small trades, some in railway, brass works, and other factories. Many were living in a new housing estate and the school was becoming overcrowded.

IV B. (i) Building very similar to IV A

A very good Junior school with mostly formal teaching, but with an atmosphere particularly happy. The classes were not overcrowded. Parents followed similar occupations to those of School IV A children.

The two schools were in the same district.

Owing to changes in this school, another was used in the second year.

10 LONG TERM TESTING IN INFANT SCHOOL

IV B. (ii) Building and parents' occupations similar to those of School IV A.

There was no overcrowding. The curriculum was well-balanced, but subjects were taught in a formal way·

V A. (ii) Number on roll—580.

The school was divided, with four classes in other buildings, which made it difficult for the staff and children to meet, as a complete school. There was good playing field attached.

Here the curriculum was divided into two parts.

1. Active, 9.0 a.m.-10.15 a.m.
Assembly and break.

2. Practice. (This was the teacher's time, to be planned as he or she chose.) Such lessons as Physical Training and Music were necessarily fixed so that all had access to the hall.

Each teacher kept a record book and in it she forecast the work which a project was likely to involve. If, however, there were any subjects which did not appear in the course of two or three weeks—as, for example, Hygiene or Nature Study—then these lessons would have a special place. This school was in the preliminary stages of breaking away from tradition. There had been many changes of staff.

V B. (ii) Number on roll—420.

This was a good modern building, but crowded. Similar to School V A. Difficulties were that classes worked in the hall, and that the playing field was away from the school.

The Infant and Junior Departments were under one Headmaster.

The Headmaster's description of the school was that it was, "more academic than activity", but they hoped to approach the younger classes through activity methods when the Head had been to a course.

CHOICE OF TESTS AND SCHOOLS 11

PILOT STUDY WITH TEN-YEAR-OLD CHILDREN

Since the battery of tests had been built up for work with nine-year-old children it was necessary to make certain that the tests were difficult enough to give full scope for ability at ten. During the year when the nine-year-olds were being tested, the same tests were administered to two classes of children aged ten. This brief preliminary study had shown clearly that the Mechanical Arithmetic Test and the Test for Ingenuity were too simple.* It was also thought necessary to experiment with some of the other tests, and a group of some 50 ten-year-olds was used in another piece of preliminary work to aid in the choice of materials and techniques and to evolve the final form of the tests to be used with the selected groups. The changes to be noted in the tests for ten-year-old children were thus arrived at.

The major differences were:

1. The Ingenuity Test with the nine-year-olds had consisted of 24 coloured shapes to be made into a picture. This was easy enough at nine years of age for a good many of the children's pictures to be put in Class 1.

A harder test had to be evolved. The test as it was used in the main part of the research was created by Miss Clare Barry, Lecturer in Education at Furzedown Training College, who undertook this part of the pilot study.

The first trials were with the original test shapes, adapted to make them more difficult and irregular, but the results showed that the test was still too easy and it was felt that less familiar materials were needed to test ingenuity with these older children.

Materials such as pins and straws were suggested, but the transport and preservation of the test material had to be kept in mind and the following materials were finally selected because they were capable of being appended to paper and were found to be used ingeniously by certain children

---

*The Mechanical Arithmetic was found to require a shorter time limit for children aged ten rather than substituting a more difficult test.

12 LONG TERM TESTING IN INFANT SCHOOL

during the pilot test while other children found the task more difficult.

4 matchsticks

6 brass headed paper clips

6 ins. of string

a piece of cotton wool, 1 in. across.

a 1 in. square of white lint.

a piece of corrugated cardboard 6 ins. x 4 ins.

a piece of black paper with white on the alternate side, 6 ins. x 4 ins.

These, it was hoped, would give variety of texture and offer scope enough for inventiveness. The size of the paper for the picture was fixed at 10 ins. x 12 ins. since the mass of material to be used would be in the right ratio to this area for filling the space pleasingly. The paper used was Dryad's elephant grey Cambridge paper and the use of this paper, the size, and that of the other materials, was rigidly adhered to throughout the research, as any deviation from the standardized size of the materials might have vitiated the test, by proving to be an advantage or handicap.

PRELIMINARY WORK ON THE MECHANICAL ARITHMETIC TEST

As with the test for children aged nine, this test was adapted from Schonell's Diagnostic Arithmetic Tests. The following table from figures in the book accompanying the tests (pp. 53-55) gives the average time in minutes taken to complete each part of these tests for children aged ten.

Type of sum	Number of Sums	Average Time Taken
Graded Addition	58	9 mins.
Graded Subtraction	56	10 mins.
Graded Multiplication	53	25 mins.
Graded Division	44	9 mins.

CHOICE OF TESTS AND SCHOOLS   13

Using these figures as a basis, a shortened form of the test was compiled, made up of :—

14 Graded Addition sums taking an average time of		2 mins. 10 secs.
14 Graded Subtraction	... ...	2 mins. 30 secs.
14 Graded Multiplication	... ...	6 mins. 30 secs.
16 Graded Division	... ...	3 mins. 20 secs.
58 Graded Sums		14 mins. 30 secs.

This gave 58 graded sums taking an average time of 14 mins. 30 secs.   30 seconds was allowed for writing the name, so that altogether the test took 15 minutes.

A rough duplicated copy was tried out with the 50 children being used in the preliminary studies.   None got all the sums right in the given time, but there was a spread of marks from 9 to 56, and it was felt this would be a fair test to use.

GENERAL COMMENTS MADE BY THE TESTERS ON
THE NINE-YEAR-OLDS' WORK

Comments were made on various matters which illustrate the point to which I have already referred, namely that the conditions for obtaining reliable results were less satisfactory this year than in the ten year olds' year which followed.

Points mentioned were :

(1)   Keen regret that the examiner had not administered a non-verbal intelligence test in schools IB and IIIB where a considerable number of children were weak in reading.

(2)   The tests were given too closely together, the work having been compressed into three days owing to the necessity of using schools so far from London.   The two examiners suggested that a third examiner should be added in the following year in order to do the work in a more leisurely fashion.   (This was done.)

(3)   Some children appeared over anxious, perhaps because the examiners had had little time to establish rapport.

14 LONG TERM TESTING IN INFANT SCHOOL

They made remarks such as, " My mummy says you must be Inspectors " or, " I expect this is a practice for the Scholarship."

(4) The examiners strongly recommended that the tests should be given again at the age of ten for the following reasons :—

(a) The difference in results might well appear more clearly at a later stage.

(b) Some of the nine year olds seemed still preoccupied with the task of adjusting to Junior School conditions, especially in the case of schools where teachers felt critical of the buoyancy of children from the experimental Infant Schools. On the other hand one examiner says,

> The results in the experimental and in the control schools were to be seen in the children themselves rather than in their work, and the clearest thing I saw after doing this piece of research was the need for Personality Tests, Sociability Tests and Attitude Tests.
>
> The children in the experimental schools were interested and interesting—they were adventurous, alive, spontaneous, unspoilt and with a rich vocabulary. They were keen to work—anxious to know the "why" of things, happy with each other and with their teachers. The children in the control schools were duller on the one hand but full of horse-play on the other, they were more difficult to handle and less keen on the work.

GENERAL OBSERVATIONS MADE BY THE TESTERS OF TEN YEAR OLDS' YEAR'S WORK

1st EXAMINER (who tested Schools IIA and B, IIIA and B, and IVA and B.)

" The Junior Schools used in this particular part of the research were all much alike in equipment, outlook and curriculum. None of these schools was doing experimental work.

The immediate and obvious difference on going in to work with the children, was their attitude. The experimental groups worked freely and serenely, and responded to a normal conversational and friendly tone (even if they were not accustomed to this in their particular class). A

CHOICE OF TESTS AND SCHOOLS 15

strange adult and rather strange things to do were accepted and enjoyed.

With the control groups it was very difficult to maintain the same natural tone, the children seemed to resent even this variation from the normal routine. In School IVB particularly the children were difficult to handle. This group in the Infant school had had a keen and enthusiastic headmistress who was untiring in her efforts to see that her ideas were carried out. In spite of, or perhaps because of this it was very difficult to get the children to say or write what they themselves would like to do.

In School IIIB the children were not so negative in their behaviour but they were used to continual direction and commands and their reaction to the different kind of adult supervision was in subdued giggling and whispering.

In School IIA and B where the control and experimental groups were mixed in the same class, the tests were begun before the children's names were known and yet after the experience of the other schools it was possible after five or ten minutes to pick out the two groups almost correctly. As with each control group there was the same fussing from a number of children over broken or lost pencils or other material and excuses to get out of the room.

Impressions in the general testing situation were that the form of some of the tests—for example the English and ingenuity tests—produced behaviour that might be the result of the kind of environment in which the children had been taught—that the experimental Infant schools had tended to foster independent thinking, adaptability and self-confidence.

The pencil and paper tests were mostly accepted unquestioningly, except the adventure story; this caused difficulty in the control groups because it had to be " out of their own heads."

The material for the Ingenuity Test induced inhibitions in some of the children which were clearly not induced in others. This was the test that showed the most immediately

16 LONG TERM TESTING IN INFANT SCHOOL

obvious results to the examiner. The experimental groups responded at once to the fun and the challenge of the material and the most usual reaction in these schools was a momentary buzz, an outbreak of chatter and queries and then, as the possibilities became evident, a quiet settling down. The control groups showed much more anxiety.

In the control schools the children seemed less at ease with the examiners except during the Intelligence and Arithmetic Tests. Even here, however, there was a great deal of fussing over filling in the front page of the Intelligence Test.

The Arithmetic in all cases was accepted without comment, the control groups in particular liked the idea of being timed and kept asking if they could have another speed test. When the Arithmetic was used for concentration the children of School IVA (experimental) thought it was a huge joke to go on doing " Hundreds and hundreds " of sums and seemed eager to do so.

In the Arithmetic tests the children in the experimental Schools generally attempted the harder problems though they did not always score marks for them. The control children were less inclined to attempt them."

2nd EXAMINERS (who tested Schools IA and B, VA and B and a third school where the numbers proved too small to be used when the children were paired.)

In the control Schools, I could not help noticing the absence of vitality in the classroom, the desire of the children to be noticed by the adult and their reluctance to work without the constant criticism and interruption of the teacher.

Such remarks as these were overheard :—
1. " I wish our ordinary school was like this."
2. (a) " After play we'll be going back to our class."
    (b) " Yes."
    (a) " What a shame !"

CHOICE OF TESTS AND SCHOOLS 17

Regret and disappointment were expressed when the days of testing were ended. To have us with them was a relief as they were pleased to be rid of their daily routine for a few days.

Usually, on the first day of our visits to the control schools the children appeared reserved, uncommunicative and astonished that they were permitted to talk quietly or hum tunes at the conclusion of a test, or even during a test like Free Drawing or Ingenuity.

In more than one school children hid from the testers (or believed they did) to whisper to other children. It was often necessary to repeat instructions, for at times they seemed unable to attend and concentrate. They failed to place their papers in the right piles (question papers and answers), and were often seen hiding their answers between other children's, fearing to place them on the top of the pile. Insecurity and failure to grasp a situation were very evident.

In some cases the freedom offered was taken advantage of by girls who giggled almost incessantly, and who apparently by so doing hoped to attract attention, or possibly expected a scolding.

In other instances, children made a nuisance of themselves by attempting to distract others from their work. This was in all cases checked to some extent. By the end of the first day, when they accepted us as their friends, then they were most helpful and friendly.

In the experimental schools it was evident that the children had some degree of freedom, greater in one than in the others.

In most cases the children showed ability to concentrate, and real interest in the work undertaken. It was interesting to note how the children here tackled the difficult problems in Arithmetic, even if they failed to get the answers accurate, there was some satisfaction in knowing that they had made a fair trial. It was also noteworthy that as the majority of pupils completed this test, they checked their results.

18 LONG TERM TESTING IN INFANT SCHOOL

The majority of them read as they completed a task and appeared to derive much pleasure by so doing.

In one school, which I felt was outstanding, the children did not wait to be told, neither did they ask any questions, but at the end of each test they quietly opened their books and began reading, never interrupting a neighbour. They regarded reading as a pleasure; it was even chosen by some as a "Free Choice of Occupation."

Here too, without being told, as the class finished a test, two of them collected test papers and written work in separate bundles. They showed a developed sense of responsibility and purpose.

They were friendly and conversed as freely and easily with us as they did with their teachers or among themselves. Some of the topics on which they conversed rather fluently and sensibly were Music, Poetry and Drawing.

Unlike the control schools I felt that their expression of sorrow and regret at our departure was personal and not merely regret at returning to their normal routine, for we heard such words as :—

1. " It was nice having you."
2. "We are sorry you're leaving so soon."
3. " You must come to see us again."

CHAPTER II

TEST I. (A)

CONCENTRATION

THE TESTS (GROUP A) IN WHICH THE AIM WAS
ASSESSMENT OF ATTITUDES TO SCHOOL LIFE
AND WORK

Purpose of the Test. In the results described in
"Testing Results in the Infant School", it was found in
three out of four pairs of Infant Schools that children in
the Experimental Schools were superior to their controls
both in concentrating on a school task of their own choice
and in performing an uninteresting task which they were
asked to do in order to help the tester. It was decided
to attempt to ascertain whether after a period in the Junior
Schools the same superiority would be found and, in order
to make the test rather more exacting for these older children, to add a third test of continuing to work on a school
task (Arithmetic) after the period allowed for the test in
this subject had expired.

TEST I. (A)

CONCENTRATION ON A TASK OF THE CHILDREN'S
OWN CHOICE

Instructions for Administering the Test. Provide children
with at least seven and not more than twelve occupations of
a sort to which they are accustomed in school. All occupations should be those which the children could continue
without completing the work in the time available.*

Show them all the materials; say, "Now you are going
to choose one of these things to play with, and you can go

*The time for all the tests of concentration was only limited
by the school period for recess. In cases where a school had
a longer period than its control, the score was made only on
the first part of the test which equalled the maximum time
allowed to the control school.

19

20 LONG TERM TESTING IN INFANT SCHOOL

on playing as long as you like, but when you are quite tired of it and you want to change, you are going to come and tell me. When you have got your things, sit down in your places and wait until I tell you to start."

When all children have chosen occupations, say, " Now begin " and note time.

After they are well started, stop them for a moment and say, " Now you can go on playing with these things as long as you like, but when you are quite tired of playing with them, come and tell me."

When children reported that they wanted to change their occupations, the tester noted the time and allowed the child to choose another occupation. In scoring the test the longest period of concentration was recorded in minutes, whether or not the longest score was for the first occupation selected.

CHILDREN'S REACTIONS TO THE TEST
Nine-year-olds
School I A

The children showed great interest, but two children who had chosen plasticine changed after five minutes. Settled at their second choice. Many children did not change at all.

School I B

The children showed great interest. One child said, " Can we draw anything?"

School II A and II B

The materials available in this school were rather limited.

" A " children

Most occupations were connected with drawing. Very little other work. Children took some time to choose and settle down. Surprisingly few changes. Some children would have gone on for much longer.

"B " children

The children were very keen to begin. Two children did not change. The teacher said that one boy who did not

TESTS (A): ASSESSMENT OF ATTITUDES 21

change may have been afraid to ask as he had a speech defect. The boy who changed most was a very intelligent child who realised that if he wanted to try all the occupations he would have to change.

School III A

Children chose quite quickly and settled very well. Much laughter when told they might choose writing or arithmetic.

School III B

These children nearly all chose drawing occupations of one sort or another and used them nearly all the time.

Schools IV A and IV B

In both schools there was a good variety of materials from which to select occupations.

School IV A. Materials

Knitting, sewing, stick printing, story books, clay, pastels, gummed paper. This took a long time to organise as the children spent some time deciding before choosing.

The children were very sorry to stop.

School IV B. Materials

Knitting, templates, clay, stick printing, story books, pastels, gummed paper and gummed shapes were provided. The children were very excited at being able to choose; at first there was dead silence and then there was a steady flow of changing. One boy said, " Can you change three times?"

General comments. It was not easy to find sufficient interesting occupations, where often drawing with various materials was the only possibility, apart from reading, writing and arithmetic. One tester reports that this limitation was the reason why some of the children did not wish to change. She says' " They were obviously not interested in such slight changes as might be made and tended to choose drawing rather than the Three R's."

22 LONG TERM TESTING IN INFANT SCHOOL

Ten-year-olds

School I A

Five occupations were selected to make conditions comparable with School I B : drawing, sewing, reading, writing and plasticine. Again drawing proved the most popular occupation; four girls chose sewing and continued for the whole period. This may have given the school an advantage over School I B where this occupation was not available. No child chose reading or writing. This tendency of the control schools to avoid the choice of reading and writing was observed in my former work with children aged 6-7 years. It also occurs in the comments of the testers of the nine-year-old children in this study.

School I B

Only five occupations could be provided which were suitable for this test :—drawing, painting, plasticine, reading and writing. The children chatted sometimes as they worked. One said, " After play we'll be going back to our own class ", and when another child agreed, said, " What a shame !"

Drawing was the most popular occupation followed by reading and painting. The longest period of concentration, 34 minutes, was given by two boys drawing with crayons. Reading was not continued longer than 20 minutes.

School III A

A group asked to work together with plasticine to make a model.

School IV A

Much work was undertaken together. Desks were turned round without fuss to make tables. Two groups worked together with pencil and paper. Two children worked out a secret code together and four wrote a play together.

All the control school children worked individually.

School IV B (i)

Children changed their occupations very frequently. Many began with a few rows of stick-printing and then changed.

TESTS (A): ASSESSMENT OF ATTITUDES 23

School V A

Half the class chose drawing with wax crayons, a few did potato printing and the rest painted. At the end of the period they asked, " Is this anything to do with the the reports?" The tester replied, " No." One boy sighed and said, " Oh, I thought we might get a couple of A's."

School V B

Two children knitted (one only for 8 minutes). All the others preferred to paint or draw. Some children copied pictures from books. Nearly all used rulers for drawing.

TEST I (b)

Concentration on a task which was not immediately interesting to the child, but which he was asked to do in order to help the Tester.

Special Purpose of Test. To test the degree to which children in the experimental schools tend to do only what they find immediately interesting and the degree to which attention wanders unless the task is one which they would freely choose to do.

In the nine-year-old year the children were asked to cut out geometrical shapes similar to those which they had previously used for making pictures in the test for ingenuity. Only two shapes were given and the task quickly became monotonous. Nevertheless some children tended to enjoy the task, perhaps because it provided a change from the normal Junior School routine, perhaps because they enjoyed the sense of doing something useful. The children did not find it very easy, as the shapes were not large and the paper thin. It was not as a rule actually found possible to use the shapes they produced.

For the ten-year-old children the task of copying class lists was given. It was thought possible that some of these might be used for the tests for sociability, but again the work was not actually used as it was thought better to give the children typed lists to eliminate difficulties in reading handwriting.

24 LONG TERM TESTING IN INFANT SCHOOL

DIRECTIONS FOR ADMINISTERING THE TEST
Nine-year-olds

Give out paper and pencils. Say, "You know the shapes you used before play—well, I want some more of them, so that I can give them to another class of children. It takes a very long time to make them, so I want you to help me. I shall give you two shapes made of cardboard. You draw round them with a pencil and then cut them out. I want you to do as many as you can, but when you are quite tired of it you may tell me and choose something else to do."

After they have started, stop them and say, " When you are quite tired of it come and tell me."

When a child asked to stop, the tester recorded the time and allowed him to choose another occupation.

Ten-year-olds

After giving the children pencils and paper, the examiner says, " We shall want lists of all your names for some work we are doing together to-morrow. Perhaps you will have time to make two, if not, write as much as you can. When you are very tired of it and really don't want to do any more, come and tell me, but go on as long as you can so that we have plenty of names for to-morrow."

The time of stopping was carefully recorded for each child.

CHILDREN'S REACTIONS TO THE TEST
Nine-year-olds
School I A

Taken very light-heartedly and eagerly. Very few found this boring. Very ready to help and assured me after some time that they could cut for hours. Raymond stopped first after 30 minutes. Many went on to end. Disappointed at stopping.

School I B

The children were keen to help, and to cut as many shapes as possible, and to do them satisfactorily. One child said,

TESTS (A): ASSESSMENT OF ATTITUDES 25

" If I put two pieces of paper together I could do two shapes at once." They chatted as they worked.

School II A and II B

Not much difference between the A and B children. Rather inclined to fuss. Asked questions which had already been answered. Afterwards seemed very pleased to cut out and to help. One child from Group A asked if they should colour the shapes to " make them better ". One boy in Group B asked whether the shapes were wanted in any particular order. Many children in Group B asked to change scissors. All the children showed eagerness to do the task well.

School III A

No comments on this—children went on cutting for a time. Did not express any views.

School III B

Children took on the task without comment. After the children had been cutting for ten minutes one boy asked to change his scissors.

School IV A and IV B

In both schools the children were very ready to take on the work. In School IV A the tester reported, " The children worked intently and with vigour. One child rubbed the skin from her finger, but continued working."

Ten-year-olds
School I A

The children asked if they could go to each other's desks to get the correct spelling of names. This was not necessary. One girl made three lists, four made two, and the rest only one.

School I B

The children chatted quietly as they made the lists. The two boys with the highest intelligence test result made three lists each.

26 LONG TERM TESTING IN INFANT SCHOOL

School V A

When the children were asked to make as many lists as they could they asked, " What for?" They made on an average two each.

School V B

Few children made more than one list.

No special comments were made by the testers on the other schools. The test was accepted in all cases quietly and readily.

TEST I (c)

After the test in arithmetic (sums) the tester said, " Stop working. Close your paper. Now you are not to do any more of the sums in the middle part of the paper. Shut it up and start those on the back, but if you are tired of doing them you may change and do some reading or writing."

When the children had been working two or three minutes they were told again that they could stop if they wanted to. Extra sheets of sums were provided for the ten-year-old children who wished to go on, as some of the quicker children finished in less than the allotted time. This was not done in the case of the nine-year-olds, some of whom finished too soon. In their case " Maximum Time " was recorded, as they would almost certainly have continued working if there had been more work to do. The problem did not occur in many cases.

The time of changing for each child was carefully recorded. In the case of children going on until the end of the period and who would obviously have gone on longer, " Maximum Time " was recorded.

Children's Reactions to the Test

Nine-year-olds. There was very little to report in the comments of the testers beyond the fact that the test was accepted quietly and cheerfully. In School II B the children were very restless, but this may have been due to the day being very hot. On the other hand, in School III A when

TESTS (A): ASSESSMENT OF ATTITUDES 27

it was equally hot the children are reported to have settled " easily and quickly ".

There were no comments of note on the reactions of the ten-year-old children.

Method of Scoring. In all the tests for concentration the number of minutes was counted for each child.

METHOD OF CALCULATING THE SIGNIFICANCE OF THE TESTS

The significance of all the tests is calculated by dividing the difference between the two sets of results by the average deviation* of the difference. The average deviation is calculated by the formula :—

$$\text{A.D. diff.} = \frac{\sqrt{A.D._1{}^2 + A.D._2{}^2}}{N}$$

A.D. diff. = average deviation of the difference.

A.D.1 = average deviation of the scores in the experimental school.

A.D.2 = average deviation of the scores in the control school.

N. = number of subjects (which in this research is always the same and not usually less than twenty in both schools in each pair).

The criterion of significance is taken to be :

$$\frac{D.}{A.D. \text{ diff.}} = 2$$

In my previous book I took the criterion of significance to be 3, but since a value between 2 and 3 means that only about 5 times in 100 would the result be due to chance, I considered that 2 could be taken as reasonably significant. Where the result came between 1 and 2, I have put a query (?) before the result, as here the chances that the

---

*The average deviation was used because it was not always possible to obtain more than twenty children from any one school who could be paired with their controls in four respects. With these rather small groups the standard deviation would be greatly affected by one or two extreme cases. The average deviation is approximately .85 of the standard deviation.

28   LONG TERM TESTING IN INFANT SCHOOL

result could be due to chance—range between 10 and 40 per cent. Results which came below 1 are labelled " insignificant."

RESULTS OF TEST I

Test (a) (Children's Choice)

School.	Result.	In favour of :
	Children aged 9	
II A & B.	.54	Insignificant.
IV A & B.	3.77	Experimental.
	Children aged 10	
I A & B.	5.31	Experimental.
II A & B.	1.39	? Experimental
III A & B.	5.39	Experimental.
IV A & B.	3.38	Experimental.
V A & B.	0	Insignificant.

Test (b) (Set task not immediately interesting.)

School.	Result.	In favour of :
	Children aged 9	
II A & B.	0	Insignificant.
IV A & B	32.36	Experimental.
	Children aged 10	
I A & B.	.45	Insignificant.
II A & B.	.37	Insignificant.
III A & B.	2.11	Experimental.
IV A & B.	2.32	Control
V A & B.	2.26	Experimental.

Test (c) (Concentration on Arithmetic)

School.	Result.	In favour of :
	Children aged 9	
II A & B.	1.55	? Control.
IV A & B.	2.46	Control.

TESTS (A): ASSESSMENT OF ATTITUDES 29

Children aged 10

I A & B.	.74	Insignificant.
II A & B.	1.84	? Experimental.
III A & B.	.07	Insignificant.
IV A & B.	4.35	Experimental.
V A & B.	.64	Insignificant.

TEST II

LISTENING AND REMEMBERING

Purpose of the test. In my first work a test was given by reading a short passage to the Infant school children describing a scene and then asking them to draw a picture putting in all the points mentioned. The object of this test was to compare the ability of children in the experimental and control schools to listen to what they were told and to remember it. In three out of four pairs of schools tested the experimental children excelled over their controls and it was, therefore, decided to see whether this superiority was maintained after two or three years in the Junior schools.

The original passage was too simple for these older children, so after preliminary experiment with more than 100 children aged nine and another 100 children aged ten, with varying degrees of intelligence, it was found that a passage taken from Eileen and Rhoda Power's " Boys and Girls of History " (Cambridge University Press) was suitable in that all children were found able to answer some questions on it, while none fully succeeded in giving all the possible details asked for.

The first story, " Lucius has a holiday ", was selected and the first 103 lines were read to the children after the instructions were given.

Instructions for Administering the Test. Give out pencils, papers and question papers face downwards. Say, " I am going to read you part of a story just once and then I am going to ask you ten questions about the story and I want you to write the answers on your papers. Listen

30 LONG TERM TESTING IN INFANT SCHOOL

very carefully, because I am only going to read it once."
Read the story. No time limit.

1. Where did Lucius keep his money?
2. How did Lucius know how much money he had?
3. How old was Lucius?
4. How old was his sister?
5. How did the Britons copy the Romans?
6. What was Lucius's father's house called?
7. What was it like?
8. How was Claudia dressed?
9. Why did she call Lucius "greedy one"?
10. What did slaves have to do?

Methods of scoring. At first it was thought that the
questions could be marked either right or wrong, but on
going through the papers it was found that this was not
possible as it seemed unfair that, for example, a child who
in answer to Question 2 wrote, "Lucius knew how much
money he had by writing down on wax tablets", should receive no more credit than the child who wrote," Lucius
knew because he wrote it down", which one felt could not
be discounted. Therefore a scale of marks for each
question was devised.

1. *2 marks*—e.g. "In an earthenware", "pot", or "jar"
or "pitcher".

   1 mark for "in a pot", "jar", etc.

2. *3 marks* for any sentence mentioning counting and
writing results on wax tablet, e.g. "Lucius knew how much
money he had by the little wax tablets he marked whenever
he put in a coin."

   2 marks for mention of use of wax tablets.

   1 mark for keeping a written account.

3. *1 mark.*
4. *1 mark.*
5. *3 marks* for mentioning giving children Roman names
and sending them to schools to learn about the Romans, etc.

   1 mark for giving names or building houses or roads.

TESTS (A): ASSESSMENT OF ATTITUDES   31

6. 1 *mark*.

7. 2 *marks* for good description mentioning either courtyard and building materials, i.e. brick, stone and plaster; or building materials and one other characteristic, e.g. mosaic floors or position of bedrooms.

1 *mark* for mention of either building materials or one characteristic.

8. 3 *marks* for full description of dress.

2 *marks* for coloured overdress and mention of bracelets or jewels.

1 *mark* for colour of dress.

9. 1 *mark*.

10. 3 *marks* for tending fires, cooking, and fetching and carrying for masters.

1 *mark* for any one activity.

Total for full score : 20 marks

CHILDREN'S REACTIONS TO THE TEST

Nine-year-olds.

School I A

Listened well. Settled down easily and well to answer questions. No real comments. Only one question—" May we answer in any order?"

School I B

All the children listened to the story. Three children finished in 10 minutes.

Schools II A and II B

All listened well. Some questions especially from the A group. " Shall we put each answer on a different line?", etc. Questions about spelling. The children were asked to do their best and reassured that no notice would be taken of spelling mistakes. To have allowed these questions would have reminded other children of points forgotten by them.

School III A

Children listened attentively. Children a long time in starting work; said, " Shall we draw a margin?", " Shall we

32 LONG TERM TESTING IN INFANT SCHOOL

leave lines between questions?"   "Shall we write the numbers of questions?"

School III B

Interrupted by violent thunder-storm.   Taken very well under the circumstances, but the sound of rain on the roof of the hut in which the class was held may have proved distracting.   The tester had to make a break in reading the story to wait for the thunder to cease and this too may have proved a handicap.

School IV A

No comments   The children quickly and quietly started work.

School IV B

The children asked about spelling, but they were told that spelling would not count.   Seven children finished after 10 minutes.

Ten-year-olds
School I A and I B.

The test was completed in absolute silence in both schools. In School I B the children sat with arms folded when their papers were completed.

School V A

Children who were over-anxious to do their best asked for spellings, although the tester had said none could be given.   This soon stopped.

School V B

As the children finished, they sat with their hands on their heads till told by the tester that they need not do so.

There were no other comments of note in the ten-year-old classes.   Apparent intentness of listening was reported generally.

RESULTS OF TEST II

School.	Result.	In favour of.
	Children aged 9	
II A & B.	1.38	? Experimental.
IV A & B.	1.97	? Experimental.

TESTS (A): ASSESSMENT OF ATTITUDES 33

Children aged 10

I A & B.	.52	Insignificant.
II A & B.	3.28	Experimental.
III A & B.	2.16	Experimental.
IV A & B.	4.4	Experimental.
V A & B.	5.5	Experimental.

TEST III. INGENUITY

Purpose of the Test. During my previous work with Infant School children it was found that one of the tests which showed the most striking superiority of the experimental schools over their controls was that of asking the children to undertake a task of which they had had no previous experience—that of using geometrical shapes to invent a picture. The shapes were not on the whole very suggestive and many of the " experimental " children showed great ingenuity in seeing possibility for their use, while the " control " children found the task much more baffling. I was eager to see whether this superiority was maintained after two or three years of Junior School education which was approximately of the same kind for both sets of children.

During the year of pilot study with nine-year-old children the same shapes were used as for the six and seven-year-olds of my previous test, but the shapes were reduced in size and owing to war-time difficulties of supply, white instead of coloured paper had to be used on a black ground made by cutting up paper supplied for " blacking out " of windows. The tests again showed superiority of the experimental schools.

For the year when the actual research began with nine-year-old children it was possible again to supply coloured shapes and this was done and may have contributed to the fact that it was found this year that the test did not appear to leave sufficient " spread ". The children found the task very attractive and the upper classes from both types of school were crowded, while few children fell below

34 LONG TERM TESTING IN INFANT SCHOOL

the standard allowed as "average". For this reason it was decided to devise a harder test for ten-year-old children. Merely increasing or decreasing the number of shapes did not appear desirable, since to increase them would almost certainly make the test easier rather than harder, while to decrease them would give little scope for a variety of pictures.

During the nine-year-old year it was decided to give two tests—one for the inventing of any picture imagined by the child and another for a definite picture asked for by the tester, selecting alternative subjects likely to appeal respectively to boys and girls. The difference between the two tests, however, was not a marked one, and so it seemed unnecessary to provide the second test in the ten-year-old year, but to devote the time thus saved to giving additional tests, which experiment with the nine-year-olds suggested to be more desirable.

Instructions for Administering the Tests at the Nine-Year-Old Level.

Test (a)

Give out newspaper for covering tables, paste and brushes, sheet of thick paper, foolscap size (for mounting).

Say, " I am going to give you these envelopes and there are some shapes inside, and when you've got your envelope, I want you to shake out the shapes and look at them. Be careful to keep them on the desk (or your side of the desk)." Pause while they get shapes out. Then say, " Make sure there aren't any more in your envelopes. They sometimes stick. You should have two of each shape." Help children to check up. When they have their shapes correctly, say, " I want you to make any picture you like with these shapes, not a pattern, a picture. Now begin."

As children finish they bring papers to tester, who writes on the pictures exactly what they say their pictures represent.

If something is obviously intended yet the child does not name it, say, " And this?"

TESTS (A): ASSESSMENT OF ATTITUDES   35

Do not press them to name every piece.
Make sure all pieces are securely fastened on paper.

Test (b)

Procedure as above, but say, " You know the pictures you made for me yesterday—well, to-day I am going to give you some more shapes.   This time I want you to make a special picture.   I want you to make either a motor-car, or a lorry, or a lady in a fancy dress."

Assessment of Tests.   The tests were mixed and submitted to three independent assessors, who did not know from which schools the pictures came. They placed the pictures in five classes, according to the following scale.

Test (a)

Class 1.   Outstandingly good picture, possessing unity. All shapes used.
Class 2.   One very good picture, but not quite up to Class 1. *Or* two separate pictures both outstandingly good. Almost all shapes used.
Class 3.   One picture, rather dull, shapes used conventionally. *Or* only a few used, *or* two fairly good pictures.
Class 4.   One fairly ingenious object, *or* two objects with shapes used very conventionally.
Class 5.   Pieces pasted on at random and named as single objects. *Or* used only as patterns.

Test (b)

Class 1.   All pieces used, to make outstandingly good shape of object required.
Class 2.   Very good shape—nearly, but not quite, as good as for Class 1.
Class 3.   Either two objects, both quite, good, *or* one object using shapes less ingeniously than for Classes 1 or 2.
Class 4.   Poor shape and dull use of shapes. *Or* more than one object badly made.
Class 5.   Random use of shapes, *or* three or more objects very badly made.

36 LONG TERM TESTING IN INFANT SCHOOL

Children's Reactions to the Tests

School I A

(a) Great surprise caused when asked to make a picture. Two children used pencils until it was explained that they must only use shapes. One child tore paper to make new shape. All very interested and wrote their "own story" under the picture.

(b) Some children said they could not make lorry or car as they had not four circles of the same size. Several girls said their ladies were in "new looks".

School I B.

(a) The children took some time to settle. Very surprised at being told "not a pattern, a picture". Several said, " I can't make a picture " The tendency of the control groups to be astonished or dismayed at the task was noted in all four schools. They expected to be asked to make patterns and took a long time to start work, often asking for different colours or shapes.

(b) The children took a long time to settle. Some tried shapes on paper before sticking them on, others gummed them on straight away.

School II A & II B

The tests were enjoyed in both groups, although some children (control group) seemed worried at not being able to make a pattern.

School III A

(a) Several questions. One child finished in about 10 minutes. All very interested.

The examples shown of the Tests for Ingenuity are selected merely on the basis of the two children concerned happening to have chosen a similar type of subject. They are, therefore, a random sample and are representative of the kind of work which was typical of that done in the schools concerned.

TEST FOR INGENUITY

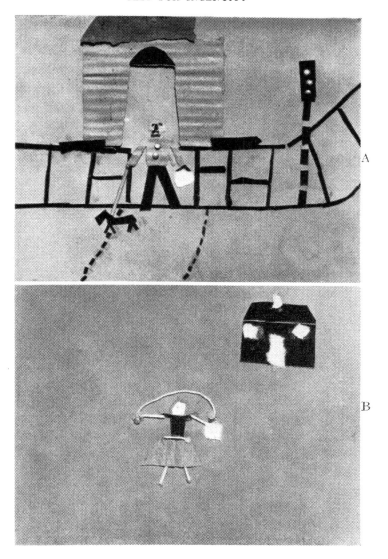

CHILDREN AGED 10
A. Experimental   B. Control

TEST FOR INGENUITY

CHILDREN AGED 10

TEST FOR INGENUITY

CHILDREN AGED 10

TEST FOR INGENUITY

A

B

CHILDREN AGED 10

FREE DRAWING

CHILDREN AGED 10

FREE DRAWING

CHILDREN AGED 10

FREE DRAWING

CHILDREN AGED 10

FREE DRAWING

CHILDREN AGED 10

TESTS (A): ASSESSMENT OF ATTITUDES 37

(b) Very restless and disturbed—took some time to settle (it was a hot day.) Finished very quickly, except for two children.

School III B

(a) At first one child used a pencil to draw his outline. He was told that pencils were not allowed in this game. Several children tried them out first before attaching the shapes to the paper. They took a long time to get started and said, " I can't think of anything—how can you make a picture?"

School IV A

The children worked without any comments for both tests.

School IV B

(a) One child said, " Can we use a pencil?" Another, " Can you draw first with a pencil?" " Can we tear the shapes?" Some tried them on the paper before sticking them.

(b) One child said, " Can you draw your lady first?"

Ten-year-olds

Instructions for Administering the Test

Test Materials

1 sheet of grey Cambridge paper 10 ins. x 12 ins. 1 envelope containing : 4 matchsticks, 6 paper clips, 6 ins. string, 1 square inch of lint, small piece of cottonwool, corrugated carboard 6 ins. x 4 ins., black paper (white reverse side) 6 ins. x 4 ins.

After the test materials are given to each child, together with scissors and glue, the examiner says : "Open your envelope and shake the things on to your paper. You have all these different things to make into a picture. You can use the black or white side of the piece of paper and there are some scissors if you want to cut, and glue to stick down your picture. Try to use everything up. Work as quickly as you can. Begin."

38 LONG TERM TESTING IN INFANT SCHOOL

The children were asked to write about their picture on the other side.

Assessment of the Test

Three independent assessors were asked to arrange the pictures in five classes. They were given the following scale :—

Class I

(i) Should have pictorial unity, an outstandingly good picture.

(ii) Should have used most of the material supplied for the test, or at least some of each material.

(iii) Should show apt and ingenious use of the material (e.g. the string used for rigging.)

Class II

(i) Should have pictorial unity, but show either :

(a) Failure to use some of each material, or

(b) Less strikingly ingenious and apt use of material.

Class III

Pictorial unity, but rather dull; most of the materials assembled in the picture, but without awareness of its possibilities.

Class IV

(i) One fairly ingenious object alone, or two or more very conventional or very dull ideas alone.

(ii) Only one material used, or different ones stuck on the mounting sheet at random round one object.

Class V

Either the material mounted at random, or only one very conventional object among random pieces, or very little material used at all.

The first assessment was made of the work of one pair of schools only, but after experiment with the results from the schools in the London area, it was considered better to assess the four pairs of schools together. In this way there was less danger of lowering the standard of judgement

TESTS (A): ASSESSMENT OF ATTITUDES   39

for one group and the assessors were never aware frɔ n which schools the pictures came. The same paper and materials were used throughout the research so that there was no distinction between schools or areas. Though the assessors had the scale to go by, they found that the unusual nature of the material used for the picture made them easy of classification and their first impressions were usually adhered to, when they classified them a second time.

CHILDREN'S REACTIONS TO THE TEST

General comments made by testers

This was the test which showed the most striking difference in the behaviour of the two groups. The experimental groups responded at once to the fun and the challenge of the material and the most usual reaction was a momentary buzz— an outbreak of chatter and questions, and then, as the possibilities of the material were realised, a quiet settling down, and finally silence reigned except for an occasional comment.

In the control schools the reaction was different. In School I B there was continuous and rather anxious questioning. "What could we do with this?" "You can't make anything with this." "We've never had to do this." "Can you push the clips through?"

In School IV B paste became a source of difficulty, although the especially clean Gripfix was bought for the purpose and taken into all schools. "I want to wash my hands", "I'm all sticky and dirty." Later I saw two brassheaded paper clips on the classroom floor. When I remarked that I must not lose any, as I needed all the spare ones for another school, immediately three or four boys came out and presented me with clips which had gone into their coat lapels instead of into their pictures.

School V B was the only control school where the children are reported as having appeared to enjoy the test. They asked, "Can we come to-morrow?", and "Do we get any reports?"

40 LONG TERM TESTING IN INFANT SCHOOL

RESULTS OF TEST III

Test (i)

School.	Result.	In favour of :
	Children aged 9	
II A & B.	.6	Insignificant.
IV A & B.	2.7	Experimental.
	Test (ii)	
	Children aged 9	
II A & B.	.3	Insignificant.
IV A & B.	.08	Insignificant.
	Children aged 10	
I A & B.	.46	Insignificant.
II A & B.	.06	Insignificant.
III A & B.	1.82	? Experimental.
IV A & B.	9.03	Experimental.
V A & B.	1.65	? Experimental.

TEST IV

SOCIABILITY

Purpose of the Test. The greater friendliness and co-operativeness of the Infant School children in the experimental schools of my first research were so marked that I very much wished to see whether these characteristics were to be seen when the children had reached the upper end of the Junior School. The question of measuring these qualities was, however, much more difficult than in my first investigation, where I was resident in or near the towns where the schools were situated and was able to train and supervise a number of students using the method of time-sampling in Infant Schools where the children were accustomed to the presence of student observers and were not suspicious of being under special observation. It is not so easy to observe behaviour in the playground without arousing curiosity in nine and ten-year-old children, and,

TESTS (A): ASSESSMENT OF ATTITUDES 41

moreover, much of their social behaviour at this age takes the form of alliance and mutual "secrets" from which adults are naturally excluded. The necessity of using schools at a distance from the residence of any of the observers made it impossible to undertake protracted observations. It is doubtful how far it is possible to measure the social attitudes of such young children by any form of group test. An attempt was made in the pilot study of nine-year-olds to measure their willingness to help their companions by setting a longer monotonous task to half the class, and a much shorter one to the other half, and telling the children that when they finished they could either go out to play or help someone else to finish first. Many of the children in both types of schools chose to help, but it was very doubtful whether the children really preferred the playground and whether they did in fact find the task monotonous, or whether the desire to win approval and feel useful to the teacher was the motive for helping rather than the desire to assist a friend. The delight in being busy and getting a job finished is very strong in children of this age, and they are not easily bored! We suspected sometimes that children who chose to go out into the playground with their friends were behaving with quite as much sociability as those who chose to remain in the classroom. It was therefore decided not to use this test.

During the year 1947-48, while the nine-year-old children were being tested, I became interested in Moreno's "Who Shall Survive?", and in Ruth Edith Hartley's study, "Sociality in Pre-Adolescent Boys." I selected items from her tests, as it was not possible to give very much time to the test and also to administer the whole battery of tests used with the nine-year-old children which I was anxious not to curtail. It was decided to ask the children to mark on the list of their classmates those children whom they would like to play with and those special friends whom they would like to have to tea, and also to mark their best friends. I also recorded and counted the number of mutual

42 LONG TERM TESTING IN INFANT SCHOOL

choices as an indication of how far the child had won the affection of the children he preferred. I was not over optimistic about the test, since it is well known that children of this age tend to change their alliances very frequently, but I thought it was possible that a cross-section taken at a particular time might show the spread of interest in and liking for many children in those children who were particularly friendly, and a more restrictive picture in those who were less interested in their fellows. I am, however, very doubtful whether it is possible to measure all that is implied in the term "sociability" without knowing the children and observing them in many situations.

Directions for Administering the Test. Sheets of paper were distributed with a complete list (typed) of names of all the children being tested, on each side, so that each child had two sets of names.
The examiner says :—

"Now you have a list with everybody's name. I want you to put a tick against the ones you would like to play with. You may tick as many as you like."

When the children have done this they write at the top of the paper, "The ones I would like to play with". The children then turn over their papers to the other list of names, and the examiner says, "Now tick all the children you would like to take home to tea."

Using another list of names, the examiner says, "Now tick your best friends."

Children's Reactions to the Test. The children in both types of school accepted the test without difficulty. They sometimes asked whether they could mark themselves as "special friends" or whether they could choose the same children again if they had already chosen them in one test. Some surprise was expressed in being invited to tick the names of girls as well as boys, and vice versa.

In Schools II A & B it was noticeable that although the experimental school children did not choose more children

TESTS (A): ASSESSMENT OF ATTITUDES 43

than the control, they were more frequently chosen by their own and also by the control group. This fact made one regret very much that it was not possible to find more schools where the experimental and control children were mingled. Had the experimental school children proved more popular in all such schools it would have been good evidence that they were socially more successful.

Method of Scoring the Test. The number of children chosen by each child was counted in each test, and also the number of mutual choices in each school.

Children who were never chosen were also counted but there were very few of these. In all schools some children appeared to be more popular than others but differences in this respect were not marked as between the experimental and control schools. The total number of children who were chosen was of course the same as the numbers of choices made. In only one case where the experimental and control children were mixed was it possible to compare in any other way the relative success of the two groups in obtaining votes. In this case Schools IIA and B there were 198 votes for Experimental and 181 for Control children, twenty experimental children obtaining more than five votes as against fourteen controls.

RESULTS OF TEST IV

Test (a)

(Special Friends)

School.	*Result.*	*In favour of :*
	Children aged 10	
I A & B.	3.26	Control·
II A & B.	1.99	? Control.*
III A & B.	2.14	Experimental.
IV A & B·	4.70	Experimental.
V A & B.	.18	Insignificant.

44 LONG TERM TESTING IN INFANT SCHOOL

Test (b)
(Friends to play with)

School.	Result.	In favour of :
	Children aged 10	
I A & B.	3.76	Experimental.
II A & B·	1.4	? Control.*
III A & B.	3.84	Experimental.
IV A & B.	4.72	Experimental.
V A & B.	4.01	Experimental.

Test (c)
(Mutual Choice)

	Children aged 10.	
I A & B.	.5	Insignificant.
II A & B.	.76	Insignificant.
III A & B.	4.32	Experimental.
IV A & B	3.33	Experimental.
V A & B.	.65	Insignificant.

*But more experimental children were chosen.

TEST V. INTERESTS

I was anxious to see whether the kind of education given in " experimental " Infant Schools, based as it is so much on the interests of the children, gave any evidence of a more mature or enriched field of interests at the Junior School stage. It was most regrettable that distance from the schools precluded me from having an opportunity to visit the children at home and to obtain by talk with them and their parents a picture of their out of school tastes and hobbies. A questionnaire addressed to children of this age is never very satisfactory, partly because children are so often handicapped by their inability to write fluently and freely and also because they tend to show their interests and critical feelings more by action than by verbal formulation. One can easily see, for example, when they are delighted or depressed by the teaching they receive; but they do not usually express these feelings when asked a general question

TESTS (A): ASSESSMENT OF ATTITUDES   45

by parents away from the classroom, and their conscious opinions tend to change when some event occurs such as discovering how to do a certain kind of sum which had previously troubled them.   "Arithmetic" then assumes a new popularity which is possibly lost again when a fresh rule presents new difficulties.   Occasionally a child was found to include the same subject on different days under both headings—"Things I would like to learn more about" and "Things I would like to stop learning".

This did not, however, occur often and I thought it best to give the tests on consecutive days to avoid the danger of children confusing the answers to the two questions on the same day.

It is almost certain that the answers given by the children did not represent anything like the full range of their views. Nevertheless they were on the whole consistent.   The chief interest of their answers is not so much in the difference between the two groups as in the light they throw on some of the interests of Junior School children in general.   The children showed no hesitation in answering and seemed quite prepared to accept the statement that no-one would mind if they said they did not like a subject.

Three of the six questions submitted were designed to discover their attitudes towards the school curriculum, and the other three to their out of school interests.   I decided to avoid the direct question—"What do you like doing out of school?"—in order to avoid, if possible, obtaining too large a number of recent "seasonal" games which, while they are in vogue, tend to exclude the thought of other interests for the time being.   I thought the questions, with their "If" quality, making some appeal to the imagination, might possibly yield a richer harvest.

INSTRUCTIONS FOR ADMINISTERING THE TEST

Set 1

When papers have been distributed, the tester says : "Here are some interesting questions for you to answer.   Say

46 LONG TERM TESTING IN INFANT SCHOOL

just what you really think. No-one will mind if you say you do not like a subject. We want to know just what you really think. You can do them in any order you like, but put the number so that we know which one you are answering."

No time limit; children who finish go on to some other occupation.

Questions—Set 1

1. What are things you would like to learn more about in school?

2. Are there any things that they don't teach children about in school that you wish they would? If so, write down the things you would like to learn about.

3. Where would you like to go for a holiday and what would you like to see?

Set 2. (*Given on the second day*)

The tester says :

" Here are some more questions for you to answer. You will remember, won't you, to write just what you really think. Put the number of the question beside your answer."

Questions—Set 2

1. Is there anything you learn in school that you would like to stop learning? If so, write down the things you would like to stop learning.

2. If you were given £1, how would you like to spend it?

3. If you were allowed to do anything you liked for a whole day in the holidays, what would you do?

Children's Reactions to the Tests

School I A

The children finished the test quickly.

School I B

Very excited and noisy—took a long time to settle down. Did not show great interest in questions. Several could not read, and only copied questions from the board.

TESTS (A): ASSESSMENT OF ATTITUDES 47

Schools II A & B

Many questions—" Can we write more than one thing for No. 1?" Can we go to a lot of places?" "Does it matter if it isn't seaside?"

Set 2—not so many questions. "Can I write a list for No 2?" "Should we spend the money on other people?". Otherwise much less fussy. (The experimental and control groups were tested together in this school.)

School III A

The children asked many questions before beginning work—e.g. "Shall we leave a line after each question?" "Can you write about more than one subject?"

School III B

The children worked without comment and did not show much interest in the questions.

School IV A

No questions asked. The children started to work after a few minutes. One child said, "If there's nothing I'd like to stop learning, shall I put that?"

School IV B

In spite of being given explicit instructions the children asked many questions, e.g. "Can we answer them in any order?" Can we write "History?"

Set II—The children spent very little time on this test—all finished after seven minutes.

Method of Scoring the Test

Set I, Questions 1 & 2, and Set 2, Question 1

The subjects mentioned by the children were grouped as follows :—

Environmental subjects : History, Geography and Nature Study.

Creative Art : Handwork of all kinds, drawing, painting, puppetry. Dramatics and dancing were included but were seldom mentioned.

48 LONG TERM TESTING IN INFANT SCHOOL

Written English :	English exercises, dictation and spelling. (Composition, reading, writing and listening to stories are recorded separately).
Science :	Chemistry, mechanics, electricity.
Music :	Singing and musical appreciation (not eurhythmics, since it was not taught in all schools).
Playing Instrument.	Piano, violin·
Physical Training :	Includes all games, wrestling and boxing.
Domestic activities :	Cookery, laundry.
Sports :	Cycling, riding, diving, swimming, car driving, acrobatics, target shooting, dirt-track racing, fishing, hiking.
Foreign languages :	French, German, Spanish, Latin.
Vocational :	Nursing, typing, building, farming, Army and Navy, veterinary science, timber stacking.

Other items are specified singly·

A few isolated examples given by individual children have not been scored. These are :—

From experimental schools—one child wanted to study " Foreign coins " and another " Magic ".

From control schools—one child wanted to study " First Aid " and another wanted to stop learning " Everything ".

Set I, Question 3

The classification of places presented no special difficulty. They fell into three divisions :—holiday resorts familiar to the children, near their own homes; London, which was not near any schools except III A & B (where only two children selected it) ; and places " Abroad ".

In the holiday resorts near their homes the seaside was

TESTS (A): ASSESSMENT OF ATTITUDES 49

most frequently chosen, and "things you would like to see"
were as follows :—

Shark.   Blackpool Tower.
Fish.
Ships and fishing boats. The launching of a ship.
    S. S. "Queen Mary".
Donkeys.   Swimming pool.
Fairs and slot machines.   Concert Party.
Fountains.   Punch and Judy.
Happy people.   Shells.
Children.   Rock being made.

Country interests were :—

Farm.   Railway goods yard.
River.   Lakes.
Horse racing.   Animals.
Dog racing.   Birds.
Tadpoles.   Flowers.
Fountains.

Two children expressed a wish to camp and to live in a
caravan.

London :—

King and Queen. Buckingham Palace.
Historical buildings.   Model railway.
Cup Final   Circus.
Zoo.   Film stars.
Mounted Police.

Abroad :—

Three children mentioned Scotland and two Ireland, and
these were classified as "Abroad" since they were very
distant from the children.

"Things you would like to see" under this heading
were :—

Pigmies.   Big game.
Grape Vines.   Bananas on trees.
Alps and lakes.   Eiffel Tower

50 LONG TERM TESTING IN INFANT SCHOOL

Schools·
Salmon in the Dee.
Scots playing football.
Statue of St. Patrick.
Historical buildings·
Skating and ski-ing.

Two children, both in experimental schools, said they would like to go round the world.

Set II, Question 2

The ways of spending money were grouped as follows:
Presents for family and friends.

" Good causes "

Toys.

(a) for creative or imaginative activity—e.g. fretwork set, dolls and their accessories, meccano, gardening tools, conjuring set, sewing box, paints.
(b) Small models, aeroplane, train set.

Pets.

Savings Bank.

Amusements.

e.g. Fair, circus, holiday, cinema (only 3 children), going in a train.

Food.

Ice-cream, sweets, meals out,

Sports and Games.

e.g. table tennis, skates, going to swimming bath, football net and pads, cricket set, riding, cycling, cycle accessories, fishing rod, tennis racquet·

Clothes and things to wear.

Fur gloves, apron, sandals, shoes, jewels.

Books.

Stationary and school equipment.

Fountain pen, satchel, drawing book, handbag, coloured inks.

Learning something.

Piano, violin, motor bicycling.

TESTS (A): ASSESSMENT OF ATTITUDES   51

Miscellaneous items each mentioned by only one child.

Xmas tree ornaments.
Cigarette cards.
Picture.   Violin.
Gramophone.   Piano.

Set II, Question 3

Ths full list of answers was as follows.

The grouping of these items is shown in the analysis of the test.

See celebrities.	Pictures.
Mills.	Play games.
Hiking.	Play cricket.
Concerts.	Nurse baby cousin.
Picnic.	Paint.
Seaside.	Inspect electric train.
Visit relations.	Play Mothers and
Country.	fathers.
Skating.	Pick flowers.
Horse riding.	Zoo.
Camping.	Watch birds.
Cycling.	Play nurses.
Weaving, sewing, etc.	Go on steamer.
Seeing farm.	Read.
Sunbathing.	Shop.
Fair.	Play with friends.
Speedway.	Go for walk.
Park.	Mind baby.
Play football.	Play houses.
Play dolls.	Play with sand.
Help mother.	Watch boxing.
Bus ride.	Canoeing.
Watch cricket.	Wash dolls' clothes.
Fishing.	Buy chicks.
Swimming.	Have meal out.
Visit goods yard.	Play with plasticine.
Motor boat ride.	Ride motor-bike.

52   LONG TERM TESTING IN INFANT SCHOOL

RESULTS OF QUESTIONS ON INTERESTS

Nine-year-olds

Set I, Question 1

"What are the things you would like to learn more about?"

Schools I A & B

There was no very marked difference in the replies given. The subjects specified were common to both schools except that one child in the control school only wished to learn more music. A greater number of wishes were expressed in the control school, 43 as against 25 in the experimental school. The greatest difference was in English where 7 children in the control school expressed a wish for more English while only 1 did so in the experimental school.

Schools II A & B

Here the number of wishes expressed was approximately equal, 30 in the experimental, 28 in the control groups. The subjects chosen were the same in both groups except that in the experimental group 3 children expressed a wish for more English, 3 for more writing, and 2 for more stories, while in the control group 1 asked for music and 2 for scripture. One child in the experimental group specified "Electricity" which was outside the scope of the question.

Schools III A & B

Here 26 wishes were expressed in the control school as compared with 16 in the experimental. The wishes in the control school were widely scattered among the subjects, very few of which brought more than one or two requests for more. Those that obtained more than two requests were :

stories—3, creative activities—6, environmental studies—7.

In the experimental school 10 out of the 16 choices were for environmental studies and 3 for creative activities·

Schools IV A & B

Again the control school expressed the greater number

TESTS (A): ASSESSMENT OF ATTITUDES 53

of wishes, 35 as against 25 in the experimental school. Their requests were for :

Arithmetic	12
Environmental studies	7
Creative activities	5
Stories	4
Writing	3
English	3
Scripture	2

The experimental school choices were in the same subjects, but fewer in number except for :

Environmental studies	8
Creative activities	7
Physical training and games	3

Summary. The greatest difference found was that the control school children appeared to want more changes (132 requests as compared with 96 in experimental schools). The least popular subject was composition, which scored only 2 votes over all the schools. The most popular subjects were, in order of priority, environmental studies, creative activities and arithmetic, with physical training and stories coming next, but after a considerable gap, 16 votes for physical training coming after 38 requests for more arithmetic. It is possible that some children did not realise that physical training and stories could " count " as " things you would like to learn more about in school ".

Set 1, Question 2

"Things they don't teach in school that you would like to learn ".

Schools I A & B

Neither school produced a large number of requests and both had individual children who mentioned games, science and foreign languages. In the control school 3 wanted the latter.

Individual children in the experimental school mentioned geometry, " Safety-First " and farming, while in the control

54   LONG TERM TESTING IN INFANT SCHOOL

school individual children mentioned playing the violin and sport (fishing). Two also asked for cooking and two for map-making.

Schools II A & B

10 children in the experimental and 19 in the control group expressed wishes· The subjects selected were the same, except that 2 children in the experimental school asked for map-making and foreign coins, while in the control 2 wanted games and foreign languages. 3 of these children also asked for vocational subjects (typing, building and nursing.)

Schools III A & B

The number of requests was almost equal between the two schools (15 experimental, 13 control). The only differences in the subjects selected were that in the experimental school 4 children asked for cycling, horse-riding or car driving and 3 for foreign languages, while in the control school 2 asked for cooking and 1 for cursive writing.

Schools IV A & B

Here there were 14 requests from the experimental and 5 from the control school. 6 children in the experimental school wanted cycling, riding and sports (target shooting and " dirt-track ") and 4 creative art of various kinds· 1 wanted cookery and 1 foreign languages. In the control school the only subject which was not also specified by the experimental was science (2 children).

Summary. The subjects asked for are arranged in order of popularity, showing the number of requests from the experimental and control schools. The differences are not great.

Subject.	Experimental School.	Control School.
Creative Arts.	9	12
Physical exercise and games.	9	8
Cycling, riding and sports.	10	2
Science.	3	7
Foreign languages.	5	4

TESTS (A): ASSESSMENT OF ATTITUDES 55

Subject.	Experimental School.	Control School.
Cookery and domestic science.	2	5
Vocational subjects.	3	3
Musical instrument.	2	3
Map making.	1	2
Safety First.	1	1
Geometry.	1	0
Cursive writing.	0	1
Gardening.	0	1
	Total 46	Total 49

Set 2 Question 1
"Things you would like to stop learning."

Schools I A & B

There was very little difference in the replies from the two schools. 14 children from the experimental and 15 from the control specified subjects which were the same and ranged widely over the curriculum. The only difference shown in the subjects disliked was that 2 children in the control school specified composition and 1 eurhythmics, which subjects were not mentioned in the experimental school.

Schools II A & B

Here there was an interesting difference in that although ·the children were in the same Junior School a considerably larger group of the control children expressed a wish to stop learning subjects (34 control as against 15 experimental). The differences were:

Subject.	Experimental School.	Control School.
Arithmetic.	5	9
Written English & composition.	4	8
Story.	2	1
Environmental studies.	0	7
Music.	0	3
School Assembly.	0	2

56 LONG TERM TESTING IN INFANT SCHOOL

Schools III A & B

Neither school expressed many subjects disliked (6 from the experimental and 9 from the control school). Composition was mentioned by 1 and story by 2 children in the control school only.

Schools IV A & B

As in Schools II A & B, there was a more marked difference in the greater number of subjects for which the control school expressed dislike (39 as against 22 in the experimental school). The differences were:

Subject.	Experimental.	Control.
Arithmetic.	6	15
Written English and Composition.	3	7
Writing	6	2
Creative Art.	0	1
Environmental studies.	1	4
Music.	1	4
Physical Training.	0	1

Summary. The control groups showed a greater number of subjects disliked, 97 as against 57 in the experimental schools.

The results are summarised again in order of popularity, those subjects producing few objections appearing first on the list.

Subject.	Experimental.	Control.
Eurhythmics.	0	1
Physical Training.	0	1
Assembly.	0	2
Singing.	3	8
Writing.	9	3
Creative Arts.	7	7
Story.	7	10
Environmental Studies.	5	15
Written English and Composition.	9	17
Arithmetic.	17	33
	Total 57	Total 97

TESTS (A): ASSESSMENT OF ATTITUDES 57

GENERAL COMMENT ON THE THREE TESTS.

The tendency of children of this age to accept school life without much conscious criticism probably accounts for the rather small number of responses. The results of the first and third test given above do, however, perhaps indicate that children from the experimental type of Infant School tend to find the Junior School curriculum more satisfying and, therefore, to express fewer wishes for a change in the curriculum.

Set 1, Question 3

"Where you would like to spend a holiday and what you would like to see."

The children's replies were analysed under headings which seemed to represent most closely the interest revealed and the results have been summarised as follows :—

Place Chosen.	Experimental.	Control.
Country or seaside near their own homes of which previous experience probably is a factor.	55	50

Motives

For pleasures, fun fairs, play, theatre, cinema, etc.	7	18
For sights of general interest.	6	2
Historical interest.		1
Interest in Nature.	12	12
Fishing, boating, or ships and other local occupations.	5	8
Place—London.	4	3

Motives

To see the Royal Family.	1	1
Historical interests.	4	2

58   LONG TERM TESTING IN INFANT SCHOOL

Place—" Abroad ".	*Experimental.*	*Control.*
(Places varied too much for any		
useful classification to be made.)	8	11

Motives

Historical interest.	1	0
Nature.	8	5
To see how people live.	2	1
For interest in transport abroad.	0	1

Summary The numbers are too small for any useful conclusions. The results were scattered over all the schools and no particular school stands out from the others. For this reason they are not reported separately.

Set 2, Question 2
" How would you spend £1."

The children's replies are arranged in order of popularity.

	Experimental.	*Control.*
Sports and Games.	14	17
Toys (creative or imaginative)	6	14
(largely dolls and accessories).		
Food.	5	12
Toys, small models.	7	8
Amusements.	9	6
(6 holidays)		
Presents for family and friends.	9	5
Savings Bank.	7	5
Books.	4	7
Pets.	3	6
Stationery and school equipment.	3	5
Good causes.	1	6
Clothes.	4	1
Learning something.	3	0
	Total 75	Total 92

Comment. The total number of items on which children appeared to want to spend money was less in the experi-

TESTS (A): ASSESSMENT OF ATTITUDES 59

mental schools. Presents to relatives and friends and Savings Bank come slightly higher on their list. They are less inclined than the controls to be interested in rather impersonal " good causes." The numbers are, however, too small to justify conclusions being drawn.

Set 2. Question 3

"How you would choose to spend a whole day."

The answers were found to group easily under the general headings set out below. Again the answers were evenly spread throughout the schools so the total results only are given.

The modes of spending the day are shown in order of popularity.

		Experimental.	*Control.*
1.	Outings, journeys and visits to relations.	25	30
2.	Sports, swimming, riding, etc.	27	18
3.	Camping, picnicking and nature rambles.	11	15
4.	" Play " and other creative occupations found for themselves	10	8
5.	Domestic occupations.	5	1
6.	Diversions and amusements.	3	3
7.	Visiting places for sights or information.	1	2

The results are not conclusive unless perhaps Nos. 2, 4 and 5, which are all occupations the child tends to engage in independently from the adult, have any significance. 42 children from experimental schools have selected these as against 27 from the control schools; but it is not possible to attribute much value to this, as it is possible that items from Nos. 1, 3 and 7 have been thought of by the child as independent activities.

60 LONG TERM TESTING IN INFANT SCHOOL

Ten-year-olds

The same tests were presented in the same manner as for the nine-year-olds. There was nothing to report on the children's reactions to the test. They worked quietly and seemed to enjoy it, except in School V B where there was a slightly anxious reaction to the first test and an attempt was made to discuss questions with other children as if they were afraid to reveal their feelings without some support.

Set 1, Question 1

" Things you would like to learn more about."

Schools I A & B

22 children in the experimental and 17 in the control school specified subjects. The subjects were scattered widely over the curriculum and in only two subjects (sewing in the experimental school, 5 children, and history in the control school, 3 children) were there more than 2 requests for any subject. Every subject except composition secured some votes.

Schools II A & B

32 children in the experimental and 43 in the control groups asked for more of subjects which were again very widely scattered. The only subjects in which the difference between the two schools was more than 2 children were :—

	Experimental.	Control.
Creative Arts.	3	6
Environmental Studies.	12	20
Physical Training and Games.	1	5

No subject entirely failed to secure votes.

Schools III A & B

43 children in the experimental and 35 in the control school voted.

TESTS (A): ASSESSMENT OF ATTITUDES 61

Differences of more than 2 children were shown in :—

	Experimental.	Control.
Arithmetic.	6	10
Creative Arts.	7	3
Environmental Studies.	19	3
Physical Exercise.	6	9

Composition was again the only subject which failed to secure a vote.

Schools IV A & B. (i) (Pilot Study)

The number of votes was exactly equal, 77 in each school. Differences of more than 2 children were shown in :—

	Experimental.	Control.
Written English.	0	3
Writing.	1	6
Creative Arts.	18	25
Environmental Studies.	29	22
Physical Exercise.	10	4
Gardening.	3	0

Schools IV A & B. (ii) (Final Study)

81 children in the experimental as compared with only 26 in the control school voted. Differences of more than 2 children were shown in :—

	Experimental.	Control.
Arithmetic.	12	2
Creative Arts.	22	3
Environmental Studies.	25	12
Physical Exercise.	8	2

Schools V A & B

The number of votes was approximately equal (39 experimental, 35 control). The only difference above 2 was in arithmetic and written English, each of which secured 3 votes from the control schools only, and environmental studies which secured 19 votes from the experimental and 14 from the control school.

62 LONG TERM TESTING IN INFANT SCHOOL

Summary of Results. The subjects have been arranged in their order of popularity. Subjects asked for, but not usually taught in the Junior Schools, have been listed separately.

	Experimental.	*Control.*	*Total.*
Environmental Studies.	112	80	192
Creative Arts	67	50	117
Arithmetic.	36	28	64
Physical Exercise.	30	22	52
Literature.	14	17	31
Written English.	7	14	21
Writing.	6	13	19
Music.	1	3	4
Composition.	4	0	4
Scripture.	1	2	3
Total	278	229	507

SUBJECTS NOT USUALLY TAUGHT

	Experimental.	*Control.*
Science (Electricity & Wireless)	6	4
Gardening.	3	0
Cookery.	2	0
Safety First.	1	0
Foreign Languages.	0	1
Morse Code.	1	0
Films.	1	0

COMMENTS. The steep rise in the demand for environmental studies and creative arts is possibly due to less time being available for these studies owing to concentration in the schools on the " Scholarship Subjects ". If this is the case the experimental school children seem to protest more. Arithmetic seems to have remained fairly popular, but there are signs that few children want more composition or written English. The very small demand that there is for composition comes from the experimental schools, but the con-

TESTS (A): ASSESSMENT OF ATTITUDES 63

trol schools show more requests for writing and written English of other kinds.

Set 1, Question 2

" Things not taught in school which you would like to learn."

Schools I A & B

No striking differences are shown either in the number of choices (10 experimental, 15 control) or in the subjects chosen, 6 control children ask for sports (skating, boxing, swimming, etc.) as compared with 2 experimental school children.

Schools II A & B

Very little difference was shown between the two groups of children.

Schools III A & B

24 experimental and 26 control school children made requests. The chief differences were :—

	Experimental.	Control.
Creative Arts not taught in their school		
(Dressmaking & clay modelling)	0	5
Sports.	4	8
Vocational subjects		
(Bricklaying & Engineering).	4	1
Science.	6	2

Schools IV A & B. (i). (Pilot Study)

There were more requests from the control school (49 as against 40).

The chief differences are :—

	Experimental.	Control.
Creative Arts not taught in school		
(including metal work)	12	16
Physical Exercises not taught in school		
(swimming and acrobatics)	4	15
Cookery and Domestic Science.	12	8
Science.	1	5

64 LONG TERM TESTING IN INFANT SCHOOL

Schools IV A & B. (ii)

Final Study.

47 experimental and 30 control children expressed wishes.
The chief differences are :—

	Experimental.	Control.
Creative Art.	12	2
Sports.	7	1
Domestic subjects.	6	13
Foreign languages.	7	1
Good manners.	0	3

Schools V A & B

11 subjects were mentioned in the experimental and 17
in the control school.

The chief differences are :—

	Experimental.	Control.
Science.	4	1
Sports.	0	8

Summary of Results. In summarising the results
answers have been omitted if they consist of subjects which
are in fact taught in school. These were inserted by some
children. It is, of course, possible that some aspects of
these subjects were taught and the children were unable
to express what they really meant. The results are given
in order of popularity.

	Experimental	Control.	Total.
Creative Arts not taught in school. (Clay modelling, dressmaking, metal work, woodwork)	35	32	67
Sports not taught in school. (Skating, boxing, swimming, acrobatics, cycling, riding, dirt-track racing, target shooting,	21	41	62
Domestic arts. (Cookery, house repairs, and " domestic science "— unspecified).	26	27	53

TESTS (A): ASSESSMENT OF ATTITUDES   65

Science (including electricity and wireless)	14	12	26
Vocational subjects. (Bricklaying, engineering, typing, nursing)	9	10	19
Foreign languages.	13	5	18
Good manners.	2	3	5
Play (unspecified).	2	0	2
Mathematics.	1	1	2
Collecting stamps	1	0	1
Collecting—unspecified.	1	0	1
Films.	0	1	1
Safety First.	0	1	1
Total	125	133	258

Comments. Differences between the two groups are not marked, except in the preference of the control group for sports of various kinds. It seems probable that what is revealed is the normal interests of ten-year-old children.

Set 2, Question 1

"Things you would like to stop learning."

Schools I A & B

Very few wishes were expressed in either school (10 experimental, 7 control) and in both cases the subjects mentioned were chiefly arithmetic and environmental studies

Schools II A & B

Here again the number of wishes was slightly more in the experimental groups, in contrast to the nine-year-old results in these schools. Differences in regard to subjects are also slight, except for :—

	Experimental.	*Control*
Environmental studies.	11	4

66 LONG TERM TESTING IN INFANT SCHOOL

Schools III A & B

The control school showed a very slightly larger number of wishes. Differences were chiefly in :—

	Experimental.	Control
Arithmetic.	3	9
Written English.	1	11
Composition.	3	7
Environmental Studies.	10	5

Schools IV A B. (i) (Pilot Study)

47 children in the experimental and 72 in the control school expressed a wish to stop learning subjects. The large difference is, however, almost certainly accounted for by the method of teaching singing in the control Junior School. It is the only case in which requests were so concentrated on one subject. For this reason it is left out of the final summary of results. Differences of more than 2 children were shown in :—

	Experimental.	Control.
Arithmetic.	10	15
Written English.	5	0
Composition.	4	0
Literature.	9	4
Environmental Studies.	10	17
Music (Singing)	2	28

Schools IV A & B. (ii) (Final Study)

38 children in the experimental and 33 in the control school expressed wishes, though two of them, " Coming to school " and " Assembly " seemed hardly within the category of things learnt in school ! Differences of more than 2 are shown in :—

	Experimental.	Control.
Arithmetic.	2	10
Written English.	1	7
Composition.	0	11
Creative Art.	5	0
Environmental Studies.	1	11

TESTS (A): ASSESSMENT OF ATTITUDES   67

Summary of Total Result. This excludes the two irrele-
vent answers mentioned above, one reference to " project "
and the music result from the one school where the dislike
was so universal as to be evidently due to very poor teaching
of the subject. Subjects are arranged in order of popularity,
those producing the fewest objections coming first.

	Experimental.	*Control.*
Physical Exercise	No objections.	
Music (except for the one control		
school omitted)	5	2
Writing.	11	5
English Literature.	14	11
Creative Arts.	13	20
Composition.	14	22
Written English.	19	18
Arithmetic.	32	47
Environmental Studies.	49	44
(Chiefly History or Geography)		
Total	157	169

Comment

The differences between the two groups are small, and are
very probably due to the method of teaching in the Junior
Schools rather than the long-distance effects of the Infant
School. Subjects disliked appear to cluster in certain
schools rather than to be widely spread. Arithmetic, where
the spread is wider, is a subject which appears to be more
disliked in the control schools, and it was also found more
difficult by these children, as is shown in the results of the
tests in the subject.

Set 1, Question 3

" Where you would like to go for your holidays and what
you would like to do."

68 LONG TERM TESTING IN INFANT SCHOOL

The experimental groups expressed a greater number of wishes, especially to visit seaside and country resorts. Other differences were not striking, but the experimental groups expressed more ideas.

Summary of Results

Places.	Experimental.	Control.
Seaside and country resorts familiar to the children.	160	75

Motives. (Arranged in order of popularity.)

	Experimental.	Control.
Pleasure.	45	39
Nature.	25	19
Sights.	29	11
Fishing, boats, etc.	17	8
Historical.	1	2
Method of transport.	0	1

Place. London.	20	14

Motives.

	Experimental.	Control.
Sights.	9	5
Historical.	2	3
Zoo.	2	3
Royal Family.	3	1
Pleasure.	0	2
Transport.	0	1

Place.

Abroad.	30	33

Motives.

	Experimental.	Control.
Nature.	7	13
Sights.	8	8
Pleasure.	5	5
How people live.	5	3
Transport.	3	6
Historical.	1	0

TESTS (A): ASSESSMENT OF ATTITUDES   69

Set 2, Question 2

" Spending £1 ".

As with the nine-year-old children, the replies are given in order of popularity. The answers were scattered fairly equally among the schools.

	Experimental.	Control.
Gifts to friends & relatives.	43	47
Clothes.	24	26
Toys.	31	16
Savings Bank.	30	11
Books, Paints, etc.	23	15
Sports equipment.	26	19
Amusements and sports.	18	14
Food.	12	16
Articles impossible to buy for £1, pianos, bicycles, etc.	5	8
" Good causes ".	1	3
Pets.	2	1
Visits.	1	0
Total	216	Total 176

The chief difference lies in the greater number of children in the experimental schools who want to buy toys and other articles for their leisure activities. There are also more who suggest saving their money.

Set 2, Question 3

" How to spend a day ".

The children's answers have been grouped under the headings which most appropriately describe them, and are arranged in order of popularity.

	Experimental.	Control.
Expeditions, walking, journeys, visits to holiday resorts or to places for information.	50	57
Sports—swimming, paddling, boating, cricket, football, tennis, horse-riding, cycling and climbing.	43	48

70   LONG TERM TESTING IN INFANT SCHOOL

Country pursuits—		
fishing, camping, picnicking, going for rambles, etc.	47	43
Amusements—		
pictures, theatres, etc.	12	15
Shopping or domestic occupations.	9	5
Walking in the park.	5	0
Going to bed.	2	1
Anti-school riots.	0	2
Going in an aeroplane.	1	0
Doing sums.	0	1
	Total **169**	Total **172**

The differences are too slight to be significant, and as with the nine-year-olds the significance relates to the natural interests of children of this age rather than to differences between the two groups.

CHAPTER III

TEST (GROUP B) OF SUBJECTS IN THE JUNIOR SCHOOL CURRICULUM.

TEST VI ARITHMETIC

The purpose of this test, and those which follow it, is to assess the child's ability in subjects of the ordinary school curriculum. As in my first book, I adapted the tests from Schonell's "Diagnosis of Individual Difficulties in Arithmetic"

Nine-year-olds

TEST (a) MECHANICAL ARITHMETIC

Content of Test

Instructions for administering the test

Give out the papers face down, and pencils. Say, " Here are some little sums for you to do. Some of them are quite easy. Write the answers on your question papers. If you can't do one sum, go straight on to the next and work as quickly as you can. Begin with the adding column, go straight down till you reach the line, then do *this* column (point to it—2nd column) then *this* (point to 3rd column) then *this*—now begin.

Record time of starting.

Content of the Paper

These are all " ADD " sums. Work across the page.

14	31	123	9	57	87	23
+ 3	+66	+45	+19	+ 7	+31	+17

		74		77	28	608
				48	103	705
401	56	56	897	32	784	33
+607	+69	+43	+497	+65	+ 9	+219

71

72 LONG TERM TESTING IN INFANT SCHOOL

These are all " SUBTRACT " or " TAKE AWAY " sums
Work across the page.

98	55	346	18	71	54	331
—3	—32	—215	—14	—2	—39	—18

316	980	180	346	364	800	891
—27	—930	—71	—284	—295	—695	—207

When you have finished this page go on to the next.

These are all " MULTIPLY " or " TIMES " sums.
Work across the page.

91	423	711	60	303	16	86
× 5	× 3	× 5	× 6	× 3	× 7	× 8

104	8050	348	4196	34	52	79
× 9	×11	×12	×11	×22	×31	×30

These are all " DIVIDE " sums.   If there is a remainder **write**
it down.   Work across the page.

4)44	2)682	3)906	4)800
5)1515	4)27	7)50	4)97
5)156	4)167	9)372	12)759
3)248	6)745	8)29643	5)25357

TESTS (B): TESTS OF SUBJECTS 73

After 20 minutes say, " Stop working. Put a ring round the last answer you have written." See that this is done. Say, " Now you may go on and finish your papers, but if you are tired of doing it you may change and do some drawing or reading or writing." Tell them where the alternative occupations are to be found. " When you want to stop doing the sums bring your paper to me." As each paper is brought, record the time of stopping.

METHOD OF SCORING

One mark to be given for each sum worked correctly. (At first it was thought that a scale of marks might be used, but it was decided that on these simple processes only one mark could be given.)

Children's reactions to the test
Schools I A & I B

The children settled down very easily and quickly. No comments. One boy in School I A finished the whole paper in 18 minutes.

Schools II A & II B

Started well—no comments. Later, in School II A, one child asked if two sums were addition. Another was perturbed because two sums had the same answer $(9 + 7$ and $7 + 9)$.

School III A

Children settled easily and quickly. No questions after explanation. Two children worked sums across paper instead of down, as explained. Very hot day.

School III B

Children very noisy to start with, but settled quite well. One boy asked, " Shall I put the answer here?" Became very restless after a short time. Very hot day.

School IV A

Children began without comment and worked intently.

School IV B

Children were anxious to take on the test after setting to work. Some children asked questions— e.g. "I've finished

74 LONG TERM TESTING IN INFANT SCHOOL

this column, shall I go on to that?" "Shall I put the remainder here?" All the children went on until they were told to stop.

TEST (b) ARITHMETIC PROBLEMS

Instructions for administering the test

Say, "Here are some little sums for you to do; some of them are quite easy. I want to see how many you can get right. On your papers you will find the numbers 1 to 40. I want you to write your answers opposite the correct numbers. If you miss one out, put a dash by that number like this—and then go on to the next." (Go round and see it is done.)

Contents of the paper

Work these sums in your head. Write down the answers at the sides.

1. In a shop there are three tops and nine balls
   How many toys are there altogether?......................

2. In a street I saw three cats, four dogs and five horses. How many animals did I see altogether?..................

3. There were nineteen sparrows on the footpath. Nine flew away. How many were left?.......................

4. Tom had twenty marbles, but lost six. How many has he now?...

5. I get four marbles for a penny. How many can I get for threepence?...

6. I have twenty-four apples to divide amongst four boys. How many should each get if they are all to have the same number? ....

7. A baker left three loaves at each of 6 houses. How many loaves did he leave altogether?........................

8. I had 6d. and spent 3½d. on sweets. How much had I left?...

9. What should I have to pay for 20 penny oranges?......

10. How many ½d. stamps could I buy for 8d?..............

11. If I had 9 more eggs, I should have 30. How many have I now?...

TESTS (B): TESTS OF SUBJECTS 75

12. I went for a bathe every day for five weeks. How many bathes did I have?..............................

13. What is the difference between 23 and 32?..............

14. I have 84 apples and want to share them equally amongst 7 boys. How many should each get?.........

15. A baker had 80 loaves. He sold 45 and then got 12 more from another cart. How many did he have then?..

16. There are 9 trees in a row. How many are there in 8 rows?..

17. Eggs are 2d. each. What should I pay for one dozen? ....

18. Mother gave me 6½d. Father gave me twice as much. How much have I now?..................................

19. A pound of jam needs 8 ounces of sugar. How many pounds of sugar will 4 pounds of jam need?............

20. I spent 2s 1d. out shopping and still have 1s 5d. How much had I at the start?..................................

21. I spent 1s. 6d. on a tie, 4s. on socks, and a shilling on a collar. How much change did I get out of 10s?......

22. Add together a half-crown, a florin, a shilling, a six-pence and three halfpence...... ....

23. At a concert 33 people paid for seats at one shilling each. How much was paid in pounds and shillings?...

24. What will 5 pounds of apples at 5d. per pound and 3 pounds of pears at 4d. per pound cost altogether?...

25. Bananas are 5 for 6d. How many will I get for 1s. 6d.? ....

26. What is left out of 1s. 6d. after buying 7 penny and 5 three-half-penny stamps?..................................

27. A piece of wire is 3 feet 6 inches long. How many pieces 1 inch long can I cut from it?....................

28. Seven fish cost 10½d. How much did each fish cost? ....

29. Butter costs 1s. 2d. per pound. How much will I have to pay for a quarter of a pound?....................

76 LONG TERM TESTING IN INFANT SCHOOL

30. How many miles shall I walk in 2½ hours at 6 miles per hour? ....

31. In a box of 100 eggs, 2 out of every 10 were bad. How many good eggs were there in the box?............

32. A lesson starts at 10.15 a.m. and lasts 40 minutes. At what time does it finish?...............................

33. The railway fare to my uncle's house is 2s. 6d. return. If I visit him 9 times a year, how much do I spend in fares?...

34. A piece of linen is 10 inches square. I am going to put lace round all sides; how much lace will I need if I allow 2 inches extra for each corner?...............

35 Jack has to travel 100 yards along a straight road to school. He goes half way and then goes 25 yards along a side street and back to fetch a friend. How far does he walk to school?...............................

36. A box is 6 inches long, 6 inches wide and 6 inches deep. How much string will I need to tie it up if the string goes round the box twice (once each way) and uses 3 inches for the knot?...........................

37. If 2 pounds of sugar cost 5d. how much will 9 pounds cost? ....

38. How many pints of milk will be needed to fill a pail which holds 4½ gallons?...................................

39. Tom starts his homework at 5.30 p.m. At five past six he has done half of it. At what time will he finish? ....

40. What is the difference between half of 4s. 8d. and a quarter of it?...

METHOD OF SCORING

One mark to be given where only one process has to be attempted. Two marks for two processes. Three marks for three processes.

TESTS (B): TESTS OF SUBJECTS 77

Children's reactions to the test

Schools I A. & I B

No comments. Some finished very quickly, others took much longer, some children going on to the end of the period. One boy said, " Does spelling count?" Later it was found that he was writing words rather than figures.

School III A

Children settled very easily. No comments. Two children finished in 15 minutes. One child asked meaning of No. 11.

School III B

The children were not quick to settle down. Tester had to say repeatedly, " Do your own work."

School IV A

No comments from the children.

School IV B

One child said, " If it (the answer) comes to a number, have you got to put the number down?" No further comments.

Ten-year-olds

TEST (a) MECHANICAL ARITHMETIC

Instructions for administering the test

After the test leaflets are distributed and the children cautioned against opening them until told to do so, the examiner says, " Open your papers. Some of these sums are quite easy. Fill the answers in on your paper. If you can't do one sum, go straight on to the next and work as quickly as you can. Work across the page, as it tells you to. Begin." As in the test for nine-year-olds, the point reached at the end of the time limit was recorded by each child.

78 LONG TERM TESTING IN INFANT SCHOOL

Contents of the test

Name ....

Age ....

School ....

Score in given time...

Add	Take-away	Multiply	Divide
15 + 2 =	15 − 6 =	9 × 6 =	14 ÷ 7 =
8 + 6 =	16 − 9 =	8 × 5 =	21 ÷ 7 =
9 + 8 =	13 − 9 =	0 × 7 =	27 ÷ 9 =
7 + 8 =	13 − 7 =	7 × 7 =	16 ÷ 8 =
9 + 7 =	14 − 5 =	12 × 2 =	32 ÷ 8 =
7 + 9 =	16 − 7 =	9 × 4 =	56 ÷ 7 =

$$401+ \quad 209+ \quad 331 \quad 635 \quad 96 \quad 87 \qquad 4\overline{)44} \quad 2\overline{)682}$$
$$607 \qquad 39 \quad -18 \quad -25 \quad \times 6 \quad \times 4$$

$$874+ \quad 635+ \quad 283 \quad 786 \quad 104 \quad 106 \qquad 3\overline{)906} \quad 4\overline{)800}$$
$$83 \qquad 944 \quad -29 \quad -58 \quad \times 9 \quad \times 7$$

$$56+ \quad 38+ \quad 839 \quad 457 \quad 8050 \quad 7004 \qquad 5\overline{)1515} \quad 4\overline{)27}$$
$$69 \qquad 86 \quad -36 \quad -63 \quad +11 \quad \times 8$$

$$77 \quad 94 \qquad\qquad\qquad\qquad\qquad 7\overline{)50} \quad 5\overline{)156}$$
$$48 \quad 83 \qquad \text{Divide}$$
$$32 \quad 76$$
$$65 \quad 59 \qquad 8\,\overline{)24643} \qquad\qquad 9\overline{)372} \quad 3\overline{)248}$$

When you have finished these sums, turn over and do the sums on the last page.

These sums were provided merely to give scope for the test in concentration so are not set out here.

TESTS (B): TESTS OF SUBJECTS 79

METHOD OF SCORING

One mark to be given for each answer given correctly.

Children's reactions to the test

The comments from all the schools were that the children settled down to work seriously and in silence. In School I A some of the children who had finished early were seen to be checking the results of their sums. The only school where any difficulty is reported was School V B, where the children were very restless after the test was finished and also made requests to leave the room during the test itself.

TEST (b) ARITHMETIC PROBLEMS

Instructions for administering the test

These are the same as those given for administering the test to nine-year-old children.

Content of the test

It was found that the problems set for the nine-year-old children allowed sufficient scope for the ten-year-olds so the same test was used.

Children's reactions to the test

School I A

There were no comments as the children worked, but afterwards they asked, "Will you tell us our marks? Who's top?"

School I B

The test was completed in absolute silence.

School V A

There was a tendency to copy in an atmosphere of competition. One boy asked, "Who got most marks?"

School V A

The testers had to restrain the children from looking at one another's work.

General comment. In three pairs of schools—II, III and IV—the children in the experimental schools were

80 LONG TERM TESTING IN INFANT SCHOOL

noticed to have attempted the harder problems more frequently than those in the control schools, who tended to leave such answers blank.

RESULTS OF TEST

Arithmetic (a) sums.

School.	Result.	In favour of :
	Children aged 9	
II A & B.	.54	Insignificant.
IV A & B.	2.22	Experimental.
*{ I A & B.	1.36	? Experimental.
III A & B.	2.33	Experimental.
	Children aged 10	
I A & B.	2.74	Experimental.
II A & B.	.30	Insignficant
III A & B.	1.48	? Experimental.
IV A & B.	5.03	Experimental.
V A & B.	.17	Insignificant.

Arithmetic (b) Problems.

School.	Result.	In favour of :
	Children aged 9	
II A & B.	.16	Insignificant.
IV A & B.	1.56	? Experimental.
	Children aged 10	
I A & B.	1.47	? Experimental.
II A & B.	.22	Insignificant.
III A & B.	.45	Insignificant.
IV A & B.	1.64	? Experimental.
V A & B.	.96	Insignificant.

*(It seemed in this case worth reporting the results from these two schools, since the pairing for intelligence was against the experimental groups, and although methods in the two experimental Infant Schools had been disturbed, they did fulfil one of the conditions of the experimental schools in that no formal arithmetic was done before the children were six and little after that age. The results certainly appear to indicate that this procedure has had favourable effects.)

TESTS (B): TESTS OF SUBJECTS 81

TEST VII. READING

For the nine-year-old children two tests were given, both taken from Schonell's book " Backwardness in the Basic Subjects."

(1) Each child was asked to read the Schonell Test R 2 for Simple Prose, reading orally to the tester in a room or corner where he was unheard by the other children. His mistakes were noted and the number of mistakes recorded. The test was perhaps rather simple, as it is intended for children under nine years five months, but it was found that few children made no mistakes.

(2) Schonell's Reading Test R 3, A, was administered to the whole class. This test was also given to the ten-year-old children.

The instructions for administering the tests are given by Schonell (Appendix 1, " Backwardness in the Basic Subjects ") and were strictly followed.

The children were spaced to avoid any possible copying from each other. In some cases the class was tested in two groups taken separately.

Children's Reactions to the Silent Reading Test

Nine-year-olds

School I A

The children worked in two sections. Both worked quickly and well.

School I B

Worked in two sections. Many of these children could not read, therefore could not do the test. Not many finished.

Schools II A & II B

No questions. The children settled very well.

School III A

Had to be taken in two parts, A and B streams. A's settled quickly and worked well—no questions asked. B's settled easily but worked more slowly than A's.

82 LONG TERM TESTING IN INFANT SCHOOL

School III B

Three boys put second column figures so close to the first that they had insufficient room for answers. Several children could not read, therefore were very bothered by the test. Many did not finish.

Schools IV A & IV B

No comment from the children in either school.

Ten-year-olds

The test was accepted without comment, except that in School I A some children asked questions instead of reading the instructions.

RESULTS OF TEST

School.	*Reading (Oral)* *Result.*	*In favour of* :
	Children aged 9	
II A & B.	1.43	? Experimental.
IV A & B.	.28	Insignificant.
	Reading (Silent)	
	Children aged 9	
II A & B.	.11	Insignificant.
IV A & B.	2.23	Control.
	Children aged 10	
I A & B.	1.58	? Experimental.
II A & B.	.13	Insignificant.
III A & B.	1.55	? Experimental.
IV A & B.	6.22	Experimental.
V A & B.	4.14	Experimental.

TEST VIII. ENGLISH COMPOSITON

Two papers were given on different days. The purpose of the first paper was to ascertain how far the children were able to use words to give an accurate description of various objects known to them, and to describe a simple process (i.e., how to find the way from their school to a

TESTS (B): TESTS OF SUBJECTS 83

well known landmark not far away from it). The purpose of the second paper was to discover :

(1) The ability of the children to compose (a) simple well constructed sentences, (b) a story, and (c) a short poem.

(2) To assess their sensitiveness in the choice of suitable words to express their thoughts vividly.

(3) By making the poem optional to test their confidence in attempting this form of writing.

Method of administering the Test. Paper and pencils were supplied. The questions were read aloud to the children and copies of the questions were also supplied.

As far as the school time-table permitted, no time limit was set. The school interval for recess was respected and also the time of closing, so that some limit was in fact imposed, but care was taken to see that the two schools which were to be compared had an equal allowance of time. Children who finished too soon selected another occupation.

Questions

Paper 1

(1) Say as clearly as you can what these words mean.

   (a) Orange   (c) Puddle   (e) Roar

   (b) Eyelash   (d) Haste   (f) Scorch

(2) How would you tell a visitor the way from your School to the Town Hall? (The Bus Garage? or whatever place was recommended by the teacher as well known to all the children).

(3) How would you describe the Town Hall? (or the place selected), so that the visitor would be sure to recognise it?

(4) If the visitor asked you what sort of place —— * is and what he could see in it, what would you tell him?

                                       *(their own town)

Paper 2.

(1) make up a sentence bringing in all three words.

      (a) horse, bigger, dog.

      (b) aeroplane, observers, telescopes.

      (c) bees, tongues, honey.

84 LONG TERM TESTING IN INFANT SCHOOL

(2) Write as many useful words as you can to describe
(a) robin.
(b) giant.
(c) the noise of a train.

(3) Make up a story with a really good adventure in it.

(4) If you like, try to make up a short poem.
Don't write one you know already but make one up.

No help was given with spelling or anything else. Children who asked were reassured, if necessary, and told that if they just did their best it was all that was necessary.

Experiment with this test during the first pilot year proved that it was sufficiently difficult both for nine and ten-year-old children. No change was therefore made for the ten-year-old tests.

Scales of Marking

Paper 1

(1) (a) Orange. Mark 0—Incomprehensible phrase, or " it is an orange ".

Mark 1—Sentence such as " it is a fruit " or " it is juicy ", i.e. *one* salient point.

Mark 2—Sentence containing *two* points—e.g. " it is a round fruit ", or " it is round and juicy ", *or* " it is a colour and a fruit ".

Mark 3—Sentence containing *three* points, e.g. " It is a round fruit, and it is juicy," *or* two of these points, plus the colour.

Mark 4—Sentence containing *four* points—*or* three qualities of the fruit, plus the colour.

Mark 5—A very good description of the fruit, containing all salient points.

(b) Eyelash. Mark 0—Incomprehensible phrase, *or* " it is a hair ".

Mark 1—Sentence containing *one* quality, e.g. description of eyelash, or location—" hairs which grow along your eyelids," *or* " it keeps dirt out of your eyes."

TESTS (B): TESTS OF SUBJECTS 85

Mark 2—Sentence containing *two* points—e.g. location and description, *or* location plus function.

Mark 3—Sentence containing *three* points, e.g. location, description and function.

Mark 4—Sentence containing description better than for 3, i.e. *good* description, plus location and function.

Mark 5—Only given for a really good all-round answer.

(c) Roar. Mark 0—Incomprehensible phrase.

Mark 1—Sentence containing *one* point—e.g. " roar means a noise ".

Mark 2—Sentence containing *two* points—e.g. " it is a loud noise ".

Mark 3—Sentence containing *three* points—e.g. " it is the loud noise lions and tigers make when they are hungry ".

Mark 4—A good description containing the noise the animals make, plus another point, e.g., " It is the loud noise some animals make when they are cross or hungry. And sometimes the wind roars when it is stormy "—or plus " An aeroplane makes a loud roaring noise when it is flying low ".

Mark 5—A very good description, containing all salient points.

(d) Scorch. Mark 0—Incomprehensible phrase—*or* inadequate use of word alone, with no explanation.

Mark 1—Sentence containing *one* point—e.g. " a scorch is a burn ", or " a scorch comes when the iron is too hot ".

Mark 2—Sentence containing *two* points—e.g. " if something is too near the fire it goes brown ", or " if you are ironing and the iron is too hot it will make a brown mark on your frock ".

Mark 3—Sentence containing *three* points—e.g. " a scorch is a slight burn. It makes a brown mark when something is too near the fire "—or " when the iron is too hot ".

Mark 4—Good description, containing *four* points.

Mark 5—Very good description giving all points.

86 LONG TERM TESTING IN INFANT SCHOOL

(e) Puddle. Mark 0—Incomprehensible phrase, *or* one giving word with no description.
Mark 1—Sentence giving *one* point, e.g., " A puddle is water ".
Mark 2—Sentence giving *two* points, e.g. " It is when water collects in a hole " or " Puddles come when it is raining and there is a hollow ", or " It is a small pool of water ".
Mark 3—Sentence containing *three* points, e.g. " It is a small pool of water left by the rain," or " It is rain water in a hole ".
Mark 4—Sentence containing four points, e.g. " It is rain water, making a small pool. It is muddy " or " dirty ".
Mark 5—A very good description giving all points.

(f) Haste. Mark 0—Incomprehensible phrase or word with no description.
Mark 1—Sentence giving *one* point, e.g., " It is to hurry," or " to be quick ".
Mark 2—Sentence giving *two* points, e.g. " When we are in a hurry and we try to be quick ".
Mark 3—Sentence containing *three* points—" Haste means quickness. It is when we go very quickly ".
Mark 4—Sentence giving good description.
Mark 5—Very good description.
N.B. In all these tests no notice is to be taken of spelling. It is the ability to express themselves which is to be taken into account. Spelling is taken into account in the original story.

Paper 2
Mark 0—Answer giving no attempt at direction.
Mark 1—An attempt at direction.
Mark 2—Fairly good directions.
Mark 3—Directions giving names of some roads, or a distinctive landmark.
Mark 4—Clear directions, with names of roads, plus some landmark.

TESTS (B): TESTS OF SUBJECTS 87

Mark 5—A really good full direction, and description of landmarks.

N.B. With ten-year-old children three classes only were used : Class I, Clear, very correct description.

Class II, Most of the directions correct.

Class III, Directions not clear.

(3) Mark 0—Answers making no attempt at description. Mark 1—A very simple description—i.e. *one* point about building to be described.

Mark 2—Description containing *two* points.

Mark 3—Answer giving *three* points (two of these can be descriptive, and the other give the position).

Mark 4—Description giving *four* points.

Mark 5—Very good description.

(4) Mark 0—Incomprehensible phrase.

Mark 1—Answer giving *one* adjective to describe town, *or one* thing which the visitor could do.

Mark 2—Answer giving *two* points—e.g. one adjective and one suggestion for visitor, *or* two adjectives.

Mark 3—Slightly better description, plus a suggested visit.

Mark 4—Good description of town, and some suggestions for a visitor.

Mark 5—Very good description of town, and suggestions for visits.

Paper 2

(1) (a), (b), (c).

Mark 0—Incomprehensible phrase, *or* no attempt at answer.

Mark 1—Sentence using only two words.

Mark 2—Answer giving three separate, good sentences.

Mark 3—Good sentence using all three words.

(2) Mark 0—Inappropriate words.

Mark 1—*One* good descriptive word, *or* two ordinary (i.e., less appropriate) words.

Mark 2—*Three* appropriate words, *or four* ordinary words.

Mark 3—*Four* appropriate words, *or five* ordinary words.

88 LONG TERM TESTING IN INFANT SCHOOL

(3) *Composition.* (Marked by 3 assessors)

Class I

(a) Story must be original in sense of not being retold as it stands in a book, or a story with which the child is familiar. The idea may be taken from a film, or a book, but there must be elements in it which the child has composed for himself.

(b) It must be complete, with a beginning and an ending.

(c) The story must be conveyed clearly to the reader.

(d) There must be considerable fluency of ideas.

(e) There must be evidence of real ability to use words well.

Class II

(a) If the story is *not original* it must be retold very well with a standard equal to, or approaching, Class 1 in all other respects.

For original stories.

(b) The story must be complete.

(c) The story must be conveyed, although there may be some gaps and inadequate expression.

(d) Fair fluency.

(e) Fair ability with words.

  or

(f) An interesting story well told, but rendered partially unintelligible by very bad spelling.

Class III

(a) If the story is *not original* it should be up to, or not far short of, Class II standards.

  If original :

(b) The story need not be complete, but it should be partially clear and evidently intended for a story.

(c) More gaps are allowable, even if they make parts of the story incoherent.

  or

(d) A short, not very interesting anecdote.

TESTS (B): TESTS OF SUBJECTS 89

or

(e) Quite a good story, rendered difficult to read by bad spelling.

Class IV

Incomplete, broken-off story—difficult to understand owing to poor wording and incoherence, yet giving some intelligible sentences. At this standard no notice is taken of whether the story is original or not.

Class V

Quite incoherent.

(4) *Original Poem*

Mark (a) Original poem showing rhyme and rhythm.
Mark (b) Attempt at a poem—one rhyme.
Mark (c) A memorised poem, or piece of prose, written out.

CHANGES IN ASSESSMENT OF STORY AND POEM FOR CHILDREN AGED 10.

For these older children some slight modifications in the method of assessing these two tests were found desirable.

Scale for assessing written stories of ten-year-olds.

Class I. *Subject matter*

1. The story must be a real adventure.
2. The situations must be convincing.

Manipulation of plot

1. There must be a definite beginning.
2. There must be a clear logical development of the plot, with no undue emphasis on one part of the story to the detriment of another.
3. There must be a " natural " ending—i.e. one which grows naturally from what has gone before and finishes the story in a satisfying way.

Style.

The story must be written in clear, fluent English which shows a sensitiveness on the part of the writer to the meaning and choice of words, and skill in their use.

90 LONG TERM TESTING IN INFANT SCHOOL

Class II. Subject matter

The story must be a real adventure, or contain some elements of adventure.

Manipulation of plot

1. There must be a definite beginning.
2. There must be clear development of the plot, though some unevenness may be allowed.
3. There must be a definite ending, unless the child has written at length and has not had time to finish.

Style.

The story must be written clearly and fairly fluently; there must be well-constructed sentences and a fairly extensive vocabulary.

Class III. Subject matter

The story may be less interesting, but must either be a real adventure or at least contain some elements of adventure, but not so clearly conveyed.

Manipulation of plot

1. There must be *either* a definite beginning *or* a definite ending.
2. There must be an attempt at clear handling of the plot, though unevenness and gaps may be allowed.

Style.

The English must be intelligible, though the style may be monotonous, the sentences short and jerky, and the vocabulary limited.

Class IV

1. There must be some attempt at elements of adventure.
2. There must be an attempt at *either* a definite beginning *or* a definite ending.
3. There must be some intelligible sentences.

Class V

A confused jumble of words which is almost or quite incoherent.

TESTS (B): TESTS OF SUBJECTS 91

Scale for assessing poems of ten-year-olds.

Class I

Beyond suspicion the child's own poem.
A good and original idea, beautifully expressed.

Class II

Form and idea adequate.

Class III

Idea sacrificed to form.   Trite.

Class IV

Form or idea completely lost.

Class V

(i) Incoherent.
(ii) A memorised contribution.

COMMENTS ON CHILDREN'S REACTIONS TO THE TESTS

Nine-year-olds.

I A. English 1

Settled well. Some questions about the name of the landmark chosen, otherwise no questions.

I B. English 1

The children asked " What do you mean by an orange?—a colour or a fruit?" Then they settled down, but many children wrote the question instead of the answer. Children chatted frequently and had to be checked.

I A. English 2

Settled down well.   Only one question, " What is a bigger?"   Seemed very pleased at being asked for a story or a poem.

I B. English 2

Some children said, " Can you tell us what observers means and what telescope means?"

92 LONG TERM TESTING IN INFANT SCHOOL

Ten-year-olds.

I A.   English 1.   No comments.

English 2.   No comments.

I B.   English 1.

Questions asked, e.g. " Can I put ' colour of fruit' for orange ?"

English 2

Work progressed quietly.   A few questions asked. " Can we put the words in any order?"   "Have you got to give the story a name ?"

Nine-year-olds

II A.   English 1

Some questions, e.g. " If a word means two things, must I write both things ?"

II B.   English 1.   No comment

II A.   English 2

Did not settle easily.   Many questions.
" Can you miss out any questions ?"
" What are telescopes ?", etc.

II B. English 2.   No comment

III A. English 1

The children attacked the work well.   Children very much taken up with formalities.   " Shall I leave a line? Write in sentences?   Rule a margin, etc. ?"

III B. (i) English 1

The difficulty in this test was to find a landmark which all the children knew.

III A.   English 2

Several questions.   " Must we use the words in the same order ?", and bothered as before by need for margins, etc. Several children wrote very long sentences for No. 1, and were very slow. One asked, " Do you mean a bird-robin ?"

TESTS (B): TESTS OF SUBJECTS 93

III B (i)   *English 2*

One child said, "What are observers?"   Another child said, "Do you mean the paper called 'Observer'?"   Another asked, "Do bees have tongues?"

IV A   English 1

The children did not ask any questions.   Later on they asked, "Shall we leave a line between questions?"   It was difficult to find landmarks which all the children knew.

IV B   English 1

One girl said, "Do you mean orange colour?"   Another asked, "What kind of orange is it?"   A boy said, "Do I just write, 'I can eat an orange'?"   The children at first seemed puzzled but they settled down and attacked the question.

IV A   English 2

One child said, "Please, Miss, what does observers mean?" otherwise no comment.

IV B   English 2

The children said, "What does observers mean?"   They seemed baffled at first, and then settled.

Ten-year-olds

IV B (ii)   *English 1*

One child said, "Do you mean orange colour or the other?"   Otherwise no comment.

English II

No questions.

Ten-year-olds

V A (ii)   *English 1*

The children were not very observant and seemed to expect to be told what to do.   Instead of noticing where the finished papers were placed they asked, "Where should I put it, Miss?"

V B (ii)   *English 1*

A tendency to talk to each other during the test. Children had to be reminded several times that this was not allowed; as they gave in their papers many children slipped theirs

94 LONG TERM TESTING IN INFANT SCHOOL

under the pile so that their work would not be seen. This seemed to indicate fear of comparison of their work with that of more gifted children.

V A (ii)   *English 2*

After clear directions they asked unnecessary questions, such as, " May I take a piece of paper?"

V B (ii)   *English 2*

Some of the children said, "Oh, we don't like compositions," but they settled down afterwards.

RESULTS OF TEST VIII

English Composition   Paper 1

School.	Result.	In favour of :
	Children aged 9	
II A & B.	.68	Insignificant.
IV A & B.	1.02	? Experimental.
	Children aged 10	
I A & B.	.53	Insignificant.
II A & B.	.34	Insignificant.
III A & B.	1.84	? Experimental.
IV A & B.	4.60	Experimental.
V A & B.	2.17	Experimental.

English Composition.   Paper II

	Children aged 9	
II A & B.	.07	Insignificant.
IV A & B.	1.02	? Experimental.
	Children aged 10	
I A & B.	1.90	? Experimental.
II A & B.	1.49	? Experimental.
III A & B.	.22	Insignificant.
IV A & B.	.72	Insignificant.
V A & B.	2.28	Experimental.

TESTS (B): TESTS OF SUBJECTS   95

Original Story.

School.	*Result.*	*In favour of :*
	Children aged 9	
II A & B.	0	Insignificant.
IV A & B.	1.08	? Experimental.
	Children aged 10	
I A & B.	.45	Insigniificant.
II A & B.	1.59	? Experimental.
III A & B.	3.95	Experimental.
IV A & B.	2.77	Experimental.
V A & B.	3.66	Experimental.

Original Poem.

	Children aged 9	
II A & B.	1.86	? Experimental.
IV A & B.	.03	Insignificant.
	Children aged 10	
I A & B.	.25	Insignificant.
II A & B.	1.59	? Experimental.
III A & B.	1.21	? Experimental.
IV A & B.	3.64	Experimental.
V A & B.	0	Insignificant.

TEST IX

Handwriting

The first twenty words of the composition on the
" Adventure Story " were used, as it was decided to assess
writing produced when the child was not particularly concerned with trying to write well. As the test was not the
first on the paper, it seemed a suitable place to see the child's
natural writing when he was neither too tired nor working
on the stimulus of beginning a fresh page. At this age it
seemed important to measure as far as possible the natural
handwriting rather than the best the child could produce

96 LONG TERM TESTING IN INFANT SCHOOL

when specially attempting to, " do his best writing ", and also to eliminate the disadvantage to the child who might be penalised by fatigue due to his readier flow of ideas as compared with the child who had less to say.

Assessment. Hildreth's Metropolitan Handwriting Scale was used by three independent assessors, whose results were found to correlate well, and so their marks were added together. The assessors were teachers accustomed to judging children's writing.

RESULTS OF TEST IX
Children aged 10

School.	Result.	In favour of :
I A & B.	2.79	Experimental.
II A & B.	.34	Insignificant.
III A & B.	.54	Insignificant.
IV A & B.	2.06	Experimental.
V A & B.	1.05	? Control.

TEST X
Free Drawing
Purpose of the Test

The test for artistic ability, like the one for ingenuity, was one in which my former investigation showed a striking superiority of the experimental schools over their controls. In these Infant Schools, however, much freedom of subject and treatment was given in the experimental schools, while more definite teaching in technique was given in the control schools. I was anxious to see whether after two or three years' teaching in the Junior Schools the greater vigour and liveliness which had characterised the work of the experimental group had been retained. As in my former tests with eight-year-old children, there was a difficulty in that in many of the experimental schools the children were accustomed to the use of paint; whereas in

TESTS (B): TESTS OF SUBJECTS 97

all the control schools pastels were the familiar medium
It was interesting that this should have been the case, since
the Junior Schools used in this study did not otherwise
differ very much in method, and it seems that some Junior
Schools, finding the children accustomed to paint, had continued to use it. Using pastel for this test seemed inevitable, since it was found too difficult for the assessors to
rate pictures fairly when some were carried out in more
attractive media, and it would have been more unfair to
ask the control groups to use paint with which they were
unfamiliar than to use pastel for the experimental groups.
This procedure, however, did probably penalise some of the
experimental schools to some extent.

The children in some experimental schools showed lack
of interest in pastels and finished their work very quickly.

Method of administering the Test

Ask the children to give out paper and pastels.

Say, " Now I want you to draw me a picture about anything you like. You can do that for me, can't you? Now
begin."

No time limit. When children finish they can get any
other occupation.

Assessment of the Test

The drawings were placed in five classes by three independent assessors. There was no way of telling from
which schools the pictures came, as the same drawing paper
and pastels were used in every case. The control and experimental results were mixed indiscriminately.

No detailed scale was given for this test. It was merely
suggested that Class 1 should consist of outstandingly good
pictures, of the artistic value of which there could be no
doubt, and that Class V should be those of no artistic value,
while the other pictures were graded between. Assessors
were chosen by virtue of their own artistic ability and were
people accustomed to taking art with children.

The assessors' results were found to correlate sufficiently
well for their ratings to be added together.

98   LONG TERM TESTING IN INFANT SCHOOL

CHILDREN'S REACTIONS TO THE TEST

Nine-year-olds

School I A

Children seemed pleased to draw a picture of own choice. Chatted to one another about pictures. Settled very easily.

School I B

The children were fussy; they said, "Can we draw in pencil first?", "I've only got eight crayons, not nine", "My crayon is long". Then they started to work.

Schools II A & II B

The children seemed unaccustomed to free work. One boy said, "Can you draw in pencil first?" Another asked if he might have a ruler. Several wondered if they might draw anything. The girls too asked many questions—"May we draw balloons?", "May I make a picture of a poem?" Settled down quite well, however. The test was taken early and the tester was therefore unable to recognise which children had come from the experimental and which from the control school.

School III A

Children fussy in setting to work. They said, "Can I use my own crayons?", "Can I draw in pencil first?", "I have no white crayons", "Can we use both sides?" Much lively interest shown. Children chattered and showed their drawings to their neighbours, and asked their neighbours what they were drawing.

School III B

Many children said, "Can I use my pencil first?"

School IV A

One child said, "Can I use my pencil first?"

School IV B

The children worked without comment, apart from a few questions—"Can you do it about winter?", "Can you draw it in pencil first?", "I can't open my box."

TESTS (B): TESTS OF SUBJECTS 99

General comment. The testers reported that in nearly all the control schools there were children who seemed dismayed at being asked to draw freehand, and some wanted to rule every line. Several of these children produced identical pictures. A lady in a crinoline was constantly drawn in one school, while in another an identical house was drawn on one side of the paper, with twin trees on the other.

Ten-year-olds

School I A

The children worked with interest and without undue fuss. This remark was true of all the experimental schools.

School II B

The children were pleased to have an opportunity of drawing what they liked. Some of them took a few minutes looking about before attempting their pictures. On the whole the drawings were attempted with timidity and the children continued to work in silence. When most of the children had finished, the tester told them that they could talk quietly, but the result was a more pronounced silence!

School III B

This was the only school in which the children were not happy during the test. Some of the girls especially kept insisting that they were not good at drawing.

School IV B (i)

The children asked several questions before they would begin—" Which way up should the paper be?", " Can we use rulers?", " Can we do it in pencil first?"

School V B

After receiving clear directions, the children asked for permission to draw objects. " May I draw a vase of flowers?", " May I draw a border round my picture?", etc. One boy wanted to copy a picture from a book and there was a general tendency to look over other children's work. (In School V A these tendencies did not occur, though child-

100 LONG TERM TESTING IN INFANT SCHOOL

ren offered to share pastels with each other. They worked happily and confidently, chatting as they worked.)

RESULTS OF TEST X

Free Drawing.

School.	*Result.*	*In favour of :*
	Children aged 9	
II A & B.	1·65	Experimental.
IV A & B.	1.83	Experimental.
	Children aged 10	
I A & B.	1.81	? Control.
II A & B.	1.54	? Experimental.
III A & B.	2.45	? Experimental.
IV A & B.	4.48	? Experimental.
V A & B.	2.24	? Experimental.

CHAPTER IV.

SUMMARY OF CONCLUSIONS

CHILDREN AGED NINE

Had it been possible to regard all the tests as reliable, I should have said that on the whole, while there has been no evidence that the free methods in the Infant School had created any handicaps, the results were inconclusive except for one School (IVA) where they were decidedly in favour of the experimental group in four tests (Arithmetic (sums), concentration on a task which was not immediately interesting, concentration on a task of their own choice, and one test for ingenuity), and tended to be superior in six more, (Arithmetic (problems), English (paper I and II), Original Composition (story), the test for listening and remembering, and free drawing), while only in two tests (silent reading and concentration on the arithmetic test) did the School IV B excel.

It would be tempting to conclude that the effects of the Infant School methods, which showed quite clearly at the top of the Infant School, appear at first to be overlaid by the Junior School curriculum, but emerge again towards the end of that period when the children are ten years old.

Since, however, only two pairs of schools could be regarded as providing reliable results (for the reasons already mentioned) and one of these was School IVA & B it is not possible to draw such a definite conclusion. It may be that a traditional Junior School, such as IVA, which receives only experimental children without the controls, tends to accept the children's attitudes to school with favourable results to them, while a school, such as IIA and B, which receives both groups, makes a more determined attempt to bring the experimental children into line, with the result that at nine years old (though not so much at

102 LONG TERM TESTING IN INFANT SCHOOL

ten) the children appear equal. It is certain that the Junior School IV A was no better than School IV B, which was an excellent school in every respect, so the superiority of the IV A children could not, I feel, have been due to being in a better Junior School.

Since the two schools which were almost certainly penalized by the Intelligence Test and by many changes of Staff were both experimental schools, it is perhaps worth noting that in the following tests three out of four experimental schools were superior to their controls, while the remaining result was insignificant :—

 Listening and remembering
 Arithmetic (sums)
 Composition (original poem)
and that in the tests for :—

 Reading (oral)
 Ingenuity (1 and 2)
 Written English (Paper 1)
two experimental schools excelled, while two results were insignificant.

Other successes were divided between experimental and control schools with certain results proving insignificant.

The only tests in which as many as two out of four control schools were superior were Free Drawing, Silent Reading, and Concentration on the Arithmetic Test.

In the Interest Test there were more requests for changes in the school curriculum from the control than from the experimental schools—132 as compared with 96.

The full table of summarised results is set out on the following page.

CHILDREN AGED TEN

The work during this year was much more satisfactory in that no handicap was created by failure to give a non-verbal intelligence test to the very few children who were unable to read at this stage; and because it was possible to obtain reliable results from five pairs of schools.

TABULATED RESULTS

Schools	Tests given under satisfactory conditions		Tests given under less satisfactory conditions	
Tests	II A & B	IV A & B	I A & B	III A & B
Concentration (a) Own choice	I	E	I	C
(b) Set task	I	E	C	?E
(c) Arithmetic	?C	C	I	I
Listening and remembering	?E	?E	I	?E
Ingenuity (a)	I	E	?E	I
(b)	I	I	?E	?E
Arithmetic (a) Sums	I	E	E	E
(b) Problems	I	?E	I	?C
Reading (a) Oral	?E	I	I	?E
(b) Silent	I	C	I	C
English Composition Paper 1	I	?E	I	?E
Paper 2	I	?E	I	I
Story	I	?E	I	I
Poem	?E	I	E	E
Free Drawing	?E	?E	C	C

104 LONG TERM TESTING IN INFANT SCHOOL

The condition mentioned previously in Schools I A and III A, of changes of staff during the children's Infant School life, could not be entirely eliminated, but it was possible to add some children from parallel classes which had been less disturbed, so that the results from these two schools can be regarded as very much more reliable than those of the previous year. The other schools had not suffered more than the normal amount of change affecting nearly every Infant School in these days.

The results can be grouped as follows :—

1. Those in which the experimental schools certainly tend to be superior.

Concentration on a task of the children's own choice.
The test for Listening and Remembering.
(Passage read).
Sociability (Friends they would like to play with).
Composition (Original story).
Free Drawing.

2. Those in which the experimental schools tend to be superior, but to a less striking degree.

Arithmetic (Sums).
Ingenuity.
Reading.
English Composition (Papers 1 and 2).
Original poem.

3. Those which show very little difference between the two groups,

Concentration on a set task which was not very interesting.
Concentration on a set task—Arithmetic.
Sociability (Special friends). (Mutual choice)
Arithmetic (Problems).
Handwriting.

There were no results in which the control schools tended to be superior.

TABULATED RESULTS

The full table of summarised results is set out below.

	IA & B	IIA & B	IIIA&B	IVA & B	VA & B
I Concentration (a) Own choice	E	?E	E	E	I
(b) Set task	I	I	E	C	E
(c) Arithmetic	I	?E	I	E	I
II Listening and Remembering	I	E	E	E	E
III Ingenuity	I	I	?E	E	?E
IV Sociability (a) Special friends	C	?C*	E	E	E
(b) Friends to play with	E	?C*	E	E	I
(c) Mutual choice	I	I	E	E	I
V Interests. See report on this test. Nothing very significant except that in the nine-year-old year more children in the Control School expressed wishes for a change in the curriculum, but at ten years old the Experimental Children wished to learn more subjects and had more ideas for their holidays.					
VI Arithmetic (a) Sums	E	I	?E	E	I
(b) Problems	?E	I	I	?E	I
VII Reading—Silent	?E	I	?E	E	E
VIII English Composition Paper 1	I	I	?E	E	E
Paper 2	?E	?E	I	I	E
Story	I	?E	E	E	E
Poem	I	?E	?E	E	I
IX Handwriting	E	E	I	E	?C
X Free Drawing	?C	?E	E	E	E

E—Experimental distinctly superior. ?C—Control tending to be superior.
?E—Experimental tending to be superior. C—Control definitely superior.
I—Insignificant.

*But a greater number of the experimental children were chosen.

106 LONG TERM TESTING IN INFANT SCHOOL

The test for Interests has been reported verbally, and did not reveal very striking differences between the two groups; and such differences as there are are set out under the test for Interests.

From the table as shown on page 105 it can be seen that out of the total of 85 results, 35 were definitely in favour of the experimental schools, 16 tended to be in favour, 28 were insignificant, 4 tended to be in favour of the controls, and 2 were definitely in their favour.

Tests VI—IX inclusive deal with subjects which frequently find a place in the scholarship examination. Out of these 40 results there are 24 in which the experimental are either superior or tend to be so, 15 are insignificant, and in only 1 does a control school tend to be superior. It is doubtful whether this test (handwriting) carries much weight in the examination.

I feel that these results justify the concluding sentence of my previous book :—

" The results of the research which I have described in this book offer evidence that the teacher of Junior School children has nothing to fear but everything to gain from Infant School methods which make use of the free activities and spontaneous interests of the children."

It is often stated by Infant School teachers that while they would like to make use of free methods and allow play as a vital part of the Infant School curriculum, they feel unable to do so because they have to consider the scholarship examination and the demands of the Junior School. This fear certainly appears to be based upon a fallacy. As far as the subjects most frequently used for the free place examination are concerned, the results are in no case superior in the control schools, while in many cases the children from experimental schools have done better.

SUMMARY OF CONCLUSIONS 107

A very important matter which still remains to be investigated is what results would be found by testing children who have not only passed through an Infant School of the experimental kind but have experienced similar methods in the Junior School itself. I hope it may be possible in due course to obtain these results.

Printed by
E. T. HERON & CO., LTD.
LONDON AND ESSEX

Printed in the United States
by Baker & Taylor Publisher Services